D1042342

Genetic
Engineering

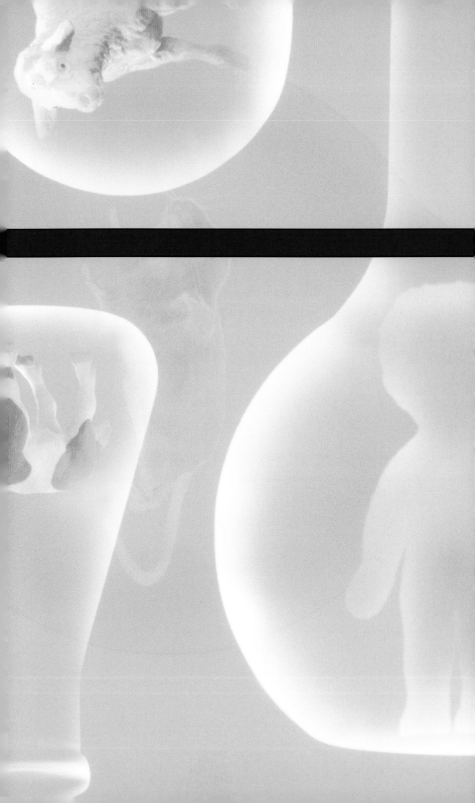

Open for Debate

Genetic Engineering

Ray Spangenburg and Kit Moser

BENCHMARK BOOKS

MARSHALL CAVENDISH
NEW YORK

With thanks to Madison Powers, J.D., D. Phil., Kennedy
Institute of Ethics, Georgetown University

Benchmark Books
Marshall Cavendish
99 White Plains Road
Tarrytown, New York 10591-9001
www.marshallcavendish.com

Library of Congress Cataloging-in-Publication Data
Spangenburg, Ray, 1939-
Genetic engineering / by Ray Spangenburg and Kit Moser.
p. cm. — (Open for debate)
Summary: Discusses the use of genetic engineering in plants and animals,
and the hopes spurred by the mapping of human DNA by the Human Genome
Project as well as the controversy over using stem cells for disease.
research.
Includes bibliographical references and index (p.   ).
ISBN 0-7614-1586-6
1. Genetic engineering—Juvenile literature. [1. Genetic
engineering.] I. Moser, Diane, 1944- II. Title. III. Series.

QH442.S694 2003
660.6'5—dc21
2002156286

Photo research by Linda Sykes Picture Research, Inc., Hilton Head, SC

William Westheimer/Corbis: Cover; Sanford/Agliolo/Corbis: 1, 2–3, 5, 102;
AP/Wide World Photos: 6, 60; Alfred Pasicka/Science Photo Library/Photo
Researchers: 16; Grant Heilman Photography: 28, 46; AFP/Tom
Kurtz/Corbis: 35; Science Photo Library/Photo Researchers: 54, 71, 77;
Bettmann/Corbis: 68; Boston Herald/Wilco/Corbis Sygma: 83; AFP/Corbis: 92.

Series design by Sonia Chaghatzbanian

Printed in China

1 3 5 6 4 2

**COVER: GENETIC ENGINEERING TOUCHES ON ALL OF LIFE—FROM CORN TO
COWS TO SHEEP TO HUMAN BABIES.**

Contents

Dolly, right, the first cloned sheep, and Polly, the world's first transgenic lamb, in their pen at the Roslin Institute in Edinburgh, Scotland, in early December 1997. Dolly later gave birth, the "natural way," to a lamb named Bonnie.

Foreword

A CLONE IN SHEEP'S CLOTHING

A sheep cloned from adult cells opens vast scientific possibilities and ethical dilemmas.

Scientific American, March 3, 1997

In February 1997, an announcement made by researchers near the city of Edinburgh, Scotland, stunned the world. It seemed simple enough. They announced that a baby ewe named Dolly had been born the previous July. But this young female sheep was special. She was a clone of her mother, a six-year-old adult sheep—the first mammal successfully cloned from an adult. Scientists had tried many times to clone animals, without success, and many people assumed it couldn't be done. Dolly was living proof that they were wrong.

Cloning admittedly steps outside the expected processes for reproduction. Dolly looks like a normal sheep. Yet she did not come from a normal egg and no sperm was involved. Dolly is an exact copy of her mother. Her mother supplied the deoxyribonucleic acid (DNA), the material in genes that provides the blueprint for building a living thing. Dolly had no father.

This may make Dolly sound like Frankenstein's monster, but she was a completely normal sheep in every way. Dolly was not stitched or bolted together, and by 1998 she became a mom herself—the usual way. After mating with a handsome Welsh mountain ram she gave birth to Bonnie, a normal, 6.7-pound (3-kg) lamb.

Sadly, Dolly had to be euthanized at the age of six on February 14, 2003, after coming down with a respiratory illness. Still, the researchers at Roslin Institute in Scotland, led by embryologist Ian Wilmut, had done the impossible. That is, they did what everyone up until that moment had thought was impossible. Other researchers had tried, and they all had failed.

Suddenly, as of 1997, genetic engineering and its ethical issues took center stage in the news. With the birth of Dolly, many "what-if" questions swiftly became much more real. Today, opinions are still many and varied—not just about cloning, its pros and cons, and the future, but also about the entire field of genetic engineering. Controversies swirl around its many faces. People are concerned about the use of genetic engineering with plants, food, viruses, endangered species, medical therapies for humans, and more. Dolly dramatically brought these questions and controversies into the public eye for the first time.

Today, public policy about genetic engineering continues to be a major area of discussion and intense debate worldwide. As scientific knowledge and skills in manipulating genes have advanced, the issues have become more and more complex. In Britain, as well as in France and other countries of the European Union, many people oppose the use of genetic engineering for improving foods. Policymakers in many countries, including the United States, are concerned about the prospect of cloning humans. In 1998, nineteen European countries signed the first binding international treaty to ban the cloning of human beings. On August 9, 2001, U.S. President George W. Bush announced his decision to limit availability of federal funds for research using human stem cells—among the first few cells developed in a human embryo—because use of these cells prevents life from forming in the embryo that supplies them.

Are some or all of these reactions too extreme? Or are they wise and ethical? Most people agree that thoughtful decisions must be made. But should the growth of this technology be stopped, as some people believe? Or should it continue with appropriate thoughtfulness and consideration? What are the cases for and against continued research and use of the various types of genetic engineering?

This book explores some of the moral, ethical, and social questions surrounding these issues. Decisions made today may well affect—for good or bad—all future citizens and inhabitants of Earth.

1
What Is Genetic Engineering?

Since Dolly's birth became public in February 1997, genetic engineering has become one of the most hotly debated topics worldwide—and it was already steamy long before that. As the noted British biologist P. B. Medawar remarked about thirty years ago, "Nothing since the early days of atomic weaponry has caused so much dismay as the real or imagined threats associated with the development of genetical engineering . . ."

The sheep Dolly was just one result of the group of various scientific processes known as genetic engineering—processes that have become the center of this intense controversy. For some critics, genetic engineering represents a threat to natural life on Earth. Other commentators hail this new field of research as the greatest, most promising breakthrough since humans harnessed electric power, or discovered how germs cause some diseases.

What's in a Name?

Some of the terms associated with genetic engineering can be confusing. People often interchange the words *biotechnology* and *genetic engineering*. The phrase *genetic modification (GM)* is another term used to describe these processes, and one of their products is genetically modified organisms *(GMO)*. Defining these terms will make it easier to discuss them.

> • *Biotechnology.* **A general term combining biology and technology. Any practical application of biological science is considered biotechnology, especially including genetic engineering and recombinant DNA technology.**

> • *Genetic engineering.* **The manipulation of genes, which are the functional units of heredity.**

> • *Genetically modified organism.* **Any living thing that has been altered at the genetic level. The organisms are also referred to as transgenic.**

You could think of genetic engineering as a tiny, microscopic construction project that takes place on very small units within living cells.

An Old Concept

In a way, genetic engineering is not really new. Farmers have controlled the outcome of plant and animal breeding since about 5000 B.C.E.—and it is still a cutting-edge field in the twenty-first century! Farmers cross-fertilized and grafted plants with different traits to obtain stronger stalks, better fruit, resistance to pests, or other improved characteristics. They also cross-bred animals. They interbred horses to increase their speed. They crossed types of chickens to improve their egg production, and they developed breeds of cattle to adapt better to certain environments.

By the late 1800s, scientists began to gain more clues about how nature did its own cross-breeding. By that time, two important figures had had some major insights into how traits are passed from generation to generation. These discoveries helped scientists to improve on methods of modifying organisms for our benefit.

Darwin and Natural Selection

In England, Charles Darwin had discovered that, through a process of natural selection, the various species of plants and animals generally adapt and improve themselves from generation to generation. They do this to survive, take better advantage of their environment, and ensure the survival of their species. He wrote about many of his ideas in a book published in 1859 titled *On the Origin of Species by Means of Natural Selection, or the Preservation of Favoured Races in the Struggle for Life*, better known as *The Origin of the Species*.

Keys to Inheritance

Meanwhile, in Austria during the years 1856 to 1863, a Catholic monk named Gregor Mendel studied what happens when many generations of peas with different characteristics are crossed. His work showed how two brown-eyed human parents can give birth to a blue-eyed child. Working with peas, he discovered that tall plants had what he called a dominant trait for tallness. When crossed with short plants, most offspring of tall plants were tall. A few, however, would be short. Why? Because all organisms carry two sets of chromosomes—one from each parent—they have sets of two genes for a trait such as eye color in humans or plant height in peas. When two genes in a set carry different instructions, one (called the *dominant* gene) may prevail over the other (called the *recessive* gene). So, the first-generation offspring of a short pea plant crossed with a tall pea plant might look tall but carry a gene for shortness as well.

Then Mendel showed that when two first-generation hybrids (with tall and short genes) were crossed with each other, an average of one out of four offspring would be short, two would look tall but carry a gene for shortness (the recessive gene) as well as the gene for tallness (the dominant gene), and one would carry two genes for tallness. In humans, brown eyes are dominant and blue eyes are recessive. So, brown-eyed parents who both have a recessive gene for blue eyes have one chance in four of producing a blue-eyed child.

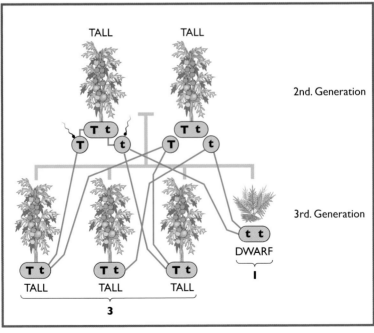

WHEN MENDEL CROSSED TWO SECOND-GENERATION PEA PLANTS, EACH WITH ONE GENE FOR TALLNESS (T) AND ONE FOR SHORTNESS (t), THE RESULTS WERE THREE TALL PLANTS AND ONE SHORT PLANT. THE ONE SHORT PLANT LACKED A DOMINANT (T) GENE FOR TALLNESS.

Better Farming through Genetics

By the 1900s, scientists and breeders alike began to pay more attention to the work of these two scientists. Today, cattle ranchers often keep careful records for many generations to produce cattle that offer more tender meat, produce better milk, or survive more successfully in a difficult environment. Other livestock (for example, chickens, sheep, and goats) and crops (such as cotton, corn, and wheat) are also raised this way. This practice is widely accepted and does not seem controversial to most people. However, it is the grandparent of genetic engineering—because it uses knowledge of genetics to manipulate the characteristics of the plants and animals that are produced.

More Insights: DNA and the Human Genome

By the mid- to late twentieth century, two more breakthroughs took place that gave scientists a greatly improved understanding of genes and how they work. First, scientists discovered the structure of the fundamental molecule that provides the key to the hereditary process—deoxyribonucleic acid (DNA). The other involved the location and identification of all the genes—the full set of genetic instructions—found in human cells.

In 1909, Danish botanist Wilhelm Johannsen (1857–1927) came up with the term *gene* to describe the idea of "hereditary elements." By the early 1950s two American geneticists, Alfred Hershey and Martha Chase, discovered that the molecule known as DNA carried the genetic information that is passed on from a parent cell to its offspring—or from a parent organism to its offspring. By 1953, two scientists working in Britain—American biochemist James Watson and British biophysicist Francis Crick—discovered the structure of DNA, a twin spiral called a "double helix." This led to a burst of growth in molecular biology—the study of the molecules that make up living things.

A few years later a Swiss microbiologist named Werner Arber found an enzyme that marked the boundaries of each gene along a strand of DNA. That discovery made the next step possible. In 1973, two American biochemists, Stanley Cohen and Herbert Boyer, used Arber's discovery to locate a specific gene in a bacterium, remove it, and place it in another bacterium. This process became known as recombinant DNA technology, or gene splicing, and it was the beginning of genetic engineering.

What Is DNA?

Every living thing is made up of cells and the products of cells. If you take a magnifying glass, you can see the cells in a plant leaf. An organism may have many different kinds of cells, making up different kinds of tissues, but nearly all cells contain a nucleus at the center. Within the nucleus we find the x-shaped structures called chromosomes, made of DNA strands all coiled up and surrounded by protein. Humans have forty-six chromosomes, and a human strand of DNA is a little over two yards long if it is pulled out and completely uncoiled. Linseed plant cells have thirty chromosomes. Bacteria are simpler, without the nucleus or the protein wrapping around the DNA, but the concept is roughly the same.

When people describe DNA's job, they commonly say DNA supplies the "blueprint" for building living things. However, that expression may be misleading. DNA is not a sketch or diagram like a blueprint. It is

THIS COMPUTER ARTWORK SHOWS PART OF A STRAND OF DNA, CLEARLY DEMONSTRATING ITS DOUBLE-HELIX STRUCTURE.

actually a physical object—a very small object, but still an object that can be broken or snapped off, just as one might break a piece of thread.

Nearly every cell in every organism contains DNA. Every cell of a mountain lion crouching in a tree, every cell of the tree, every bacterium, and every mouthful you eat of a tomato contains DNA. It does not matter whether the lion was born in a zoo or in a mountainside cave. It does not matter whether the tomato came from an organic farmer at a produce market or from a large corporation's warehouse. It still has DNA in its cells.

Physically, a gene is a section of DNA.

A gene is a unit of biological information. You might say that DNA is the recipe book and a gene represents one recipe in the book. Each gene builds a particular protein.

The ingredients for the gene's recipe are floating around in the cell—they are called amino acids. (Amino acids make up two groups of about twenty different molecules that are commonly found in every living cell.) The gene carries the instructions for putting them together in a structured pattern to form a chain of amino acids that make up a particular protein, such as an enzyme that starts chemical processes going. All the traits of any organism—your brother, a bacterium, that mountain lion—are created by the presence or absence of a particular protein. The full set of a living thing's genetic information is called the genome, and every cell of an organism contains the same genome.

This becomes obvious if you snip off a few leaves from a Swedish ivy plant, stick each leaf stalk in a small pot of damp soil, and then cover the whole thing with a plastic cap. In a few days, new Swedish ivy plants spring up from the detached leaves—showing that the instructions for growing the whole plant were present in the cells of the planted leaves.

As many as 20,000 different proteins may be present

in a single cell. Each one has a different job and is the creation of a different gene recipe. The human genome consists of some 60,000 to 90,000 genes. These different recipes give humans the ability to build all those proteins.

However, each individual organism is different, with subtle differences in its DNA. All DNA is made up of four bases arranged in different sequences. These sequences are identical in identical twins (twins that come from the same egg). Otherwise, differences exist in every individual human's DNA. Yet the language of DNA is understood by all living things. A mouse cell can read the instructions from a gene inserted from a human. A human cell understands recipes recorded in a gene from a mouse.

The following four points provide some keys to understanding how genetic engineering works. Molecular geneticist Alan McHughen calls these points "the four fundamental pillars of genetics."

1. Organisms are made up of cells and cell products.

2. Each cell contains the full genome of the organism. Skin cells, for example, contain the same genetic information as liver cells. However, liver cells do not ordinarily make skin cells and vice versa. That is because many of the recipes available in differentiated, or specialized, cells do not get read. Therefore, if a recipe is not useful to a specialized cell's purpose, it is not expressed.

3. All the genetic information necessary for creating an entire organism is contained in the genome. Therefore every cell has the recipes for creating the organism. A clone can be made—as Ian Wilmut's team did in Scotland—by starting with a cell from a sheep's udder.

They produced a clone from this cell, which grew from a single cell into a baby lamb and finally an adult ewe.

4. Every organism on Earth shares the same genetic language—DNA. This means that a gene from a mouse can be planted in a human cell and the human cell has no problem understanding the gene's recipe. And if a mouse gene is implanted into a plant cell, the plant cell understands the mouse gene's recipe. For twenty-five years a human gene inserted into a bacterium has created insulin used by people with diabetes, and the process has saved countless lives.

What's That Again?

So now, let's go back and take another look at genetic engineering. By the early 1970s, researchers had found they could introduce changes in genes. Genes, the carriers of heredity, contain the instructions for building proteins, the complex molecules that make up all living things. Each protein molecule contains many carbon and hydrogen atoms, as well as atoms of oxygen, nitrogen, and often sulfur and a few other elements. These atoms form different arrangements for each different molecule—building such proteins as hormones, enzymes, and immunoglobulins. The proteins created by genes are responsible for every trait in any plant, animal, or virus—any living thing.

Using genetic engineering, researchers insert new instructions into a cell's DNA. These instructions tell the cell how to make a specific protein. After building the protein, the cell passes these instructions on to its offspring, so they also follow the new recipe. Scientists can use this basic technique in several different ways.

This book first explores the uses of genetic engineering in the production of plants, both for foods and for other purposes. Then it takes a look at the uses of genetic engineering on members of the animal kingdom. Finally, it explores the possibilities for saving lives, curing genetic disease, and other biomedical uses for humans.

Big Issues, Tough Decisions

Genetic engineering has become a profoundly emotional issue. Whatever side they are on, people hold passionate opinions. The passion is understandable, but intense emotions can make thinking clearly about a complex issue all the more difficult. How does anyone sort through all the powerful arguments both for and against the various facets of genetic engineering?

Richard Feynman, winner of the 1965 Nobel Peace Prize in physics, once pointed out how important it is to keep from fooling oneself. This is an especially important point when trying to sort through these arguments. These are big issues:

- **the well being or starvation of millions of people;**

- **the safety of the food we eat;**

- **the ethical issues regarding the use of embryonic cells;**

- **the diversity of species on our planet; and**

- **the essence of what it means to be human.**

These are all powerful arguments used either for or against genetic engineering. For the most part, their intent is to convince others of what they believe is right—not to fool people. Yet, some arguments about genetic engineering may be biased, careless, poorly thought through, and uninformed. Additionally, these issues are highly charged emotionally—and that's when it becomes very easy to fool oneself.

Now let's embark upon a fascinating journey—an exploration of the promising possibilities, varied and often valid concerns, and ever-intriguing perplexities brought about by what may seem like science fiction but in fact is reality: genetic engineering.

2
What Are We Having for Dinner?

LABELING SETS OFF A FOOD FIGHT

Scientific American, March 3, 1997

Remember Jack and the beanstalk? A few magic seeds, planted carefully, and watch out! A beanstalk so huge it reached the skies. So, why would anyone grow genetically engineered crops—or genetically modified (GM) crops, as they are frequently called.

To start with, farming is hard work, and many obstacles stand in the way of planting, growing, and harvesting fields of soybeans, rice, corn, or any other crop. Pests destroy young plants, or weeds choke them out. Vine-ripened tomatoes bruise and damage easily and quickly rot on their way to market. So, one big set of reasons for GM crops is that genetic engineering can keep pests away, make weed control easier, and improve the shelf life of a crop so the grower can get the crop to market before it spoils. Also, GM crops can offer consumers added nutrients and vaccines against diseases.

A few GM foods have entered the U.S. marketplace without much fanfare. Some 68 percent of all soybeans sold in the United States are GM crops. Other common GM foods include corn, potatoes, canola, papaya, and squash. In general, GM crops have all been modified genetically by replacing a gene in the nucleus in order to enhance or introduce various favorable traits. Just as Mendel cross-pollinated his pea plants to produce tall ones or short ones, genetic engineers have produced different kinds of GM variations.

How much attention do people pay to what they eat? Unless a person has severe allergies, who gives much thought to the ingredients in the lunchtime sandwich, the safety of the lettuce in a Caesar salad, or the exact ingredients in the taco shells from the corner fast-food restaurant. Sometimes, though, people have become very concerned and the media has given a lot of attention to these issues. Since the 1990s, several scares have made people nervous—*E. coli* in hamburger and sprouts, fear of mad cow disease in beef, and the hazards caused by the use of bovine growth hormones (BGH) in dairy cows.

Tomatoes: An Early Debut

In 1994, the U.S. Food and Drug Administration (FDA) issued its first approval to market a genetically modified food—the Flavr Savr tomato, developed by Calgene, Inc., a biotechnology company located in Davis, California. After two years of careful, controlled testing, the FDA ruled that Flavr Savr tomatoes were as safe for eating as their traditionally developed counterparts. A public meeting was then held by outside experts who were members of the FDA's Food Advisory Committee. These panel members agreed that all relevant safety issues had been considered and resolved. The approval followed an earlier FDA approval in 1990 of the first biotechnology food product, chymosin, a milk-clotting agent for making cheese.

Calgene was pleased. The company was responding to a need for winter tomatoes that not only looked ripe, but also had good flavor. Many people find that tomatoes in supermarkets may look more or less ripe but have no taste. Commonly harvested green to protect from bruising, on arrival at market these tomatoes are usually sprayed with ethylene, the natural substance that causes ripening in tomatoes on the vine. This treatment gives tomatoes that rosy, ripened look. But they are actually still unripened. Vine-ripened tomatoes look good and taste great but they bruise easily and rot quickly. Many are lost by the time they reach market. The softening process that occurs as tomatoes ripen is controlled by a particular gene. So, Calgene's Flavr Savr tomato was manipulated using an antisense RNA that inhibited that gene and kept it from functioning. That is, the tomatoes' ribonucleic acid (RNA)—which usually drives the cells' protein production—is also programmed to silence the gene for ripening. The tomatoes looked good, tasted good, and did not rot.

The FDA testing had covered five basic questions:

1. Does insertion of the DNA into the tomato genome (the total genetic material of the tomato) change the tomato in any way that disqualifies it as food?

2. Are the measured levels of toxin within acceptable ranges? That is, are they within ranges accepted for traditionally developed tomatoes?

3. Are products produced by the antisense RNA safe for the consumer and safe for the environment? Is

there any danger of reactions within the digestive system or interactions with orally administered antibiotics?

4. Is the genetically modified Flavr Savr tomato safe for human consumption?

5. Do taste and nutrition offered by this tomato compare favorably to the naturally grown tomato?

Flavr Savr tomatoes passed all these tests. At the time FDA Commissioner David A. Kessler, M.D., stated, "We have approached our review of this product with scientific rigor and a commitment to full, public disclosure of that science. Consumers can be confident that we remain committed to assuring that foods produced by genetic engineering are as safe as food in our grocery stores today."

In 1997 the Flavr Savr tomato was also approved by Health Canada for sale as food in Canada.

However, many people were not at all sure. A public outcry ensued, objecting to the FDA approval of Flavr Savr tomatoes. They did not like the interference with nature. Questions arose. Would tomatoes now be different? How? Could they be dangerous? What about allergies? What changes were there in nutrition? What about toxins? Was the environment endangered by this newly modified food crop? Could there be a transfer of genes across different organisms?

StarLink Corn—And Taco Trouble

In September 2000, GM crops hit the news headlines in a big way when a consumer group requested a recall of a large batch of taco shells. The group had discovered that this batch of taco shells from a Mexican taco shell plant allegedly

Flavr Savr Update

As it happened, the Flavr Savr tomato had unexpected problems in shipment. Apparently, the much-touted tomato turned out to be more delicate and easily damaged than expected, requiring special trucks, and the transportation became too expensive. For the time being, the Flavr Savr issue was closed. By 1997, Calgene withdrew it from the market.

Advocates against GM foods hailed the withdrawal as a victory, but probably it was just the result of poor planning. The issues remained to return another day. By 2002, the updated version of Flavr Savr was under development by a group of researchers headed by Jim Giovannoni at the Boyce Thompson Institute for Plant Research, based at Cornell University in Ithaca, New York. Like the original Flavr Savr, when these tomatoes are picked off the vine, they are firm and red—but hardier and ready to travel. By controlling the genes that cause ripening, says Giovannoni, he and his team have found they can keep the tomato on the vine longer, where it can increase its nutritious value, while developing more attractive color and better flavor. They also reported that they expected the technique to work as well on fruits such as strawberries, bananas, and melons.

contained a genetically engineered corn known as Star-Link corn—a GM crop that has been approved by the U.S. Environmental Protection Agency (EPA), but not for human consumption. The taco shell recall did take place, but not before some people ate them, and about forty people reported symptoms of a possible allergic reaction to the Centers for Disease Control. The accident turned out to have no major consequences, but it highlighted one of the big concerns over GM crops: What happens if a GM crop gets mixed in with non-GM produce?

"StarLink," also known as Bt corn, has a special property—it grows its own pesticide. This idea may conjure up visions of chomping into a serving of corn on the cob and tasting snail bait, but the pesticide contained in StarLink is nothing like the pesticides used in backyard gardens. The name "Bt" is shorthand for *Bacillus thuringiensis*, a bacterial pesticide used by organic farmers. StarLink corn is a genetically modified organism (GMO) carrying a gene that generates a pesticide—but the pesticide is organic.

The reason StarLink corn is not approved for humans is that the genes for Bt create a protein called Cry9c. Some humans find this protein more difficult to digest than proteins naturally occurring in corn. The rule of thumb used by the regulating agencies is that a food must not contain any ingredient that might make it react in the human body in a different (and possibly unexpected) way from the original organic food. So Starlink corn was approved for consumption only as animal feed.

By mistake, some of the StarLink corn had become mixed in with the regular corn and was included in some of the tacos shipped from this particular manufacturing plant. Although a few people asked to be tested for an allergic reaction to the taco shells, no reaction could be definitively traced to the StarLink corn. The problem produced a good deal of concern for more than one reason. The international involvement placed some of the taco shell ingredients outside the jurisdiction of U.S. regulatory agencies and caused global concern over the GM scene. Also of concern was that several different kinds of corn—including both traditional and Bt corn—were stored together by a Texas miller involved in the incident.

Roundup-Ready Soybeans

Soybeans that have been bioengineered to resist herbicides have become especially popular because it makes controlling weeds so much easier. Farmers can spray their fields with weed killer without harming their crops in the process. In 2001, 80 percent of the soybean farmers in Kansas and South Dakota planted GM soybeans. Overall, as of 2001, the United States accounted for over two-thirds of all biotechnology crops planted globally.

The creator of Roundup-Ready soybeans is Monsanto, which is headquartered in St. Louis, Missouri. The company has run some 1,800 analyses comparing these GM soybeans to traditional soybeans, checking proteins, fatty

FAST-GROWING WEEDS LIKE THOSE OVERTAKING THIS CORNFIELD PRESENT A SERIOUS PROBLEM TO FARMERS, WHO OFTEN END UP RESORTING TO HERBICIDES—EVEN THOSE THAT ARE BANNED—TO KEEP FROM LOSING THEIR CROPS.

acids, and many other substances for their potential effects on humans. The results showed no differences in effects between the two kinds of soybeans.

In addition to weed-killer-resistant soybeans, numerous other crops come in herbicide-proof varieties, including cotton, sugar beets, and lettuce. Monsanto has also been working on Roundup-Ready wheat, but U.S. wheat farmers are less than enchanted. They fear contamination via cross-pollination from GM fields to traditional fields, and they are concerned that the wind could literally blow away their livelihood.

For or Against?

Most of us eat GM foods every day without even knowing it and suffer no apparent ill effects. In fact, it is estimated that more than half of our processed foods, such as breakfast cereals, contain GM soy, corn, and canola oil. These often subtly modified crops can offer improvements on nature that make growing these crops more economical, which in turn makes them more affordable to consumers. Sometimes, as in the case of tomatoes and cantaloupes, they can offer better quality for the consumer.

However, organic farmers, consumer advocacy groups, medical consultants, environmentalists, and consumers have some legitimate concerns. Government agencies have tried to address these concerns, but have they succeeded? How great are the consequences if they fail?

Pluses

- **In an era in which millions of people, especially in underdeveloped countries, suffer from hunger and malnutrition, GM crops offer a way to make inexpensive, nutritious food widely available.**

• Many farmers and agricultural scientists support the development of **GM** crops that are easier and more economical to grow.

• Genetic engineering can be used to improve the foods we eat, introducing improved flavor and nutrition.

• Careful review and testing by government agencies are already in place, and they are proceeding cautiously. Checks and balances can help guarantee unbiased, honest decisions that support the public's health and welfare.

Minuses

• **GM** foods may not be safe for everyone. What about allergies? What if government testing and controls are not good enough? What about unforeseen side effects that may show up years later?

• **GM** crops may cross-pollinate with non-**GM** crops via wind or insect dispersal, and **GM** seeds may become mixed with non-**GM** seeds. Once the crops are mixed, people will no longer be able to choose what they eat.

• The introduction of technology into a part of nature as fundamental as the gene seems unnatural, and, partly because **GM** is relatively new, this makes people uneasy.

• Some people object to genetic engineering on religious grounds, regarding it as an interference with God's creation. For those people, this fundamental objection applies to all forms of biotechnology.

3
Biotechnology as World Fare

LET'S NOT GO BANANAS OVER GENETICALLY ALTERED FOODS

"The Healthy Skeptic," e-facts.com

Since the 1960s, consumers have become more and more aware of the issue of safe food. Following the publication of *Silent Spring* by Rachel Carson in 1962, a movement toward organically grown foods and similar concerns gained strength. A heightened awareness of human effects on Earth's fragile environment also stems from that time. A marine biologist, Carson observed that DDT and other pesticides were polluting the waters and fields. Repeated exposure to these toxic substances was causing deaths and deformities, especially in birds and fish.

Then in the 1980s and 1990s, outbreaks of mad cow disease (bovine spongiform encephalopathy, or BSE) in cattle caused human deaths related to eating infected beef.

Many more people became frightened about commercial food and its safety—especially in the United Kingdom and Europe, where more than ninety people died of the disease.

No one wants to think the food we eat is unsafe. So, when it comes to growing and selling food, many countries now have strict rules and regulations about food safety. The United States is no exception, and the U.S. Environmental Protection Agency (EPA) is charged with reviewing the safety of the pesticide substances in bioengineered plants. The Food and Drug Administration (FDA) and the U.S. Department of Agriculture (USDA) also coordinate regulation in other areas of food crop certification.

Organic and GMO-Free Foods: A Luxury?

Prince Charles of Wales is an outspoken defender of organic foods and foods that are free of genetically modified organisms (GMO-free). He keeps a large organic garden for raising foods untainted by pesticides, synthetic fertilizers, or weed killers. It certainly contains no genetically modified (GM) foods. However, it is easy for Prince Charles to speak out for organic foods and GMO-free foods. His organic garden is managed by a large team of gardeners who are paid by the state. Organic gardening requires a lot of labor. Weeds have to be pulled. Worms have to be picked off tomato plants by hand.

Many of the shortcuts that make foods more affordable cannot be used in organic gardening. What does an organic dairy or beef cattle rancher do when a cow gets sick? Giving her antibiotics is out. More than likely, some of these cows die for lack of medical attention. Deaths in a herd cause a strain on the grower's costs. Those costs have to be passed on to those who choose organic foods. As one reporter put it, "In this world, what would consumers prefer to swallow: genetically engineered lettuce or more expensive salads?"

Some GM critics point out, though, that organically raised cows usually don't need antibiotics as much as their GM cousins may. The organic group does not usually have high rates of infection, while, at least among dairy cows, use of bovine growth hormone (BGH), injected to increase milk production, correlates highly with the incidence of mastitis and udder infections.

Made by Monsanto, BGH was approved in 1993 by the FDA, and is being injected into some 500,000 dairy cows. Opponents argue that the hormone causes health problems in cows. This in turn leads to the increased need for antibiotics, residues of which end up in the milk people drink.

Prince Charles and others have the right to choose organic foods, and new USDA labeling for organic foods makes shopping easier for American consumers. Frequently, these labels also indicate when food is GMO-free. This labeling offers the reassurance some consumers want, while to other shoppers these precautions seem unnecessary. Labeling, of course, cannot assure absolute safety. Even organic foods are not necessarily free of food-borne toxins, and natural fungal toxins commonly infest organic crops, which are not sprayed to prevent them. Botulism can lurk in a jar of improperly sealed home-canned beans, whether or not they are organic.

GMOs versus World Hunger?

In counterpoint to labeled inorganic and GMO-free foods, misunderstandings and political strain over GM foods produced a set of tragic results in 2002. Millions of people in Africa were dying of starvation while their government officials attempted to gauge the risks—not only to those who ate the food in their country, but also to the purity of their countries' exported crops. Unsure whether GM food was safe, and concerned over contamination of their own crops, they continued to delay.

Ironically, people were starving in Zimbabwe in southern Africa and Zambia in south-central Africa, while stockpiled GM grains sat useless in granaries in the United States. Through the World Food Program, the United States offered the food to help relieve conditions in these two countries. However, both countries refused help at first.

Zimbabwe had refused to accept the grain because officials were afraid that in the long run GM grains might contaminate crops native to their country. If farmers mixed the seeds together, the non-GM strains would no longer be pure. Not only were they not sure they wanted their people to grow and eat GM crops, the economic problem went much deeper than that. Zimbabwe exports agricultural products to European countries, where GM crops are actively shunned as inferior and many markets will not buy them. If Zimbabwe's crops became tainted with GM strains, markets for their crops could easily dry up.

Zambian officials also worried about the European market for their crops. However, they realized that grinding the seed would make it impossible to use in planting but still useful as food. This was an important point to the Zambian economy. In the same way that U.S. regulators require that StarLink corn seed must not be mixed with non-GM corn seed, Zambian officials wanted to make sure that the U.S. grain would not be mixed with their non-GM grain.

However, the United States refused to grind the corn, and other countries accused the United States of trying to force acceptance of GM crops. Meanwhile, the United Nations World Food Program (WFP) arranged to have it ground. Even so, while 3 million Zambians went hungry, the government refused to accept the corn. Since Zambia refused it, the WFP shipped the corn to countries such as Malawi and Mozambique, where officials have decided to accept the GM corn after it is ground up.

Many European nations supported the decisions made by their African suppliers. Several environmental groups have taken the stand that underdeveloped countries should

ACTIVISTS DRESSED UP AS CLONES OF PRESIDENT GEORGE W. BUSH PROTEST AGAINST GENETICALLY MODIFIED FOODS.

interesting question in his book *Pandora's Picnic Basket: The Potential and Hazards of Genetically Modified Foods.* He wonders how "Mr. Happy's Hotdog Stand" could respond to a law requiring labeling. Labeling takes time and is costly. These regulations could easily put "Mr. Happy's Hotdog Stand" out of business and place a heavy burden on food suppliers, small grocery stores, and restaurants.

Generally, GM food labeling is not as big an issue in the United States. Few restaurants along the Atlantic seaboard and in the Midwest guarantee non-GM fare. But in the San Francisco Bay area, diners can choose from some 200 restaurants that claim to be GMO-free.

In early October 2002, an article published by the *Sacramento Bee* reported that the FDA was pressuring organic food distributors to remove labels on their packaging that indicated the products are GMO-free. According to the FDA, the label implies that genetically modified ingredients are inferior to those that are not genetically modified. Members of the organic community, such as Spectrum Organic Products, Inc., put a lot of effort into making sure their products do not contain any bioengineered or even processed ingredients. Spectrum, based in Petaluma, California, says their buyers sometimes travel as far as France to obtain canola oil that can be guaranteed as GMO-free. The FDA, though, is not convinced. What about traditional selective breeding methods, when crops with ideal traits are bred together? Isn't this GM, too? And can producers and distributors be sure their products contain nothing produced in this way?

By mid-October 2002, the U.S.D.A. established a new label for organic foods. After years of campaigning on the part of organic food producers and distributors, "USDA Organic" labeling had finally arrived. Many concerned shoppers want to be sure that the produce they buy has not been sprayed with pesticides, doused in weed killers, or encouraged with synthetic fertilizers. They want to know that meats and poultry have not been treated with antibiotics or hormones. However, many different labels have been used in the past: "pesticide-free," "natural," and "organic," for example. Shoppers were not sure what the labels meant because there was no standard. Now they know that the food producers have been inspected and are all judged by the same standards.

However, GMO-free labeling is not part of the picture, and so far, FDA guidelines do not require the labeling of GMO products. Part of the agency's position is that the "USDA Organic" label gives organic growers the economic advantage of attracting customers who want to buy food that they know is free of pesticides and other interventions in the natural growing process. At the same time, consumers know that the USDA Organic foods do not contain GMOs. So, if they want to be sure of purchasing GMO-free food, they can buy USDA Organic foods.

Many people still want GMO labeling, though. Some are against GM foods because they believe them to be connected with large, corporate farming and big business. However, today, smaller farmers are also growing GM products because the potential for a bountiful harvest is so much greater and the risk of crop loss so much less.

Some GM Foods Get the Nod

In any case, only a few GM foods have so far been approved for human consumption in the United States— about a dozen as of late 2002. However, those include tomatoes, soy, canola oils, and corn, and the last three are used in about half of all the processed food we eat. These crops are engineered to resist damage from handling, weeds, or pests. They have been carefully tested, according to the FDA, and the ingredients have proved fully as safe to put on the dinner table as crops grown without genetic engineering.

Nineteen countries already require designation of GM ingredients in their labeling. The European Union has banned the sale of any new engineered products since 1998—which effectively blocks U.S. exporters of GM foods. The move has also stopped the growth of biotechnology food firms in Europe.

People in the United States have not been as strongly opposed to GM foods. In Oregon in November 2002, a proposition appeared on the ballot that would have required labeling of all foods and ingredients produced through biotechnology—which, of course, included genetic engineering. By that time, though, the new USDA Organic regulations were already in place, providing consumers with at least some of the information they needed. Oregonians voted the measure down.

At the end of his book, *Pandora's Picnic Basket*, Alan McHughen leaves his readers with this comment:

> **Constant media coverage of food scares notwithstanding six billion people eat something every day without undue harm to themselves or the environment. The tragic incidents of harm from food are extremely rare. This doesn't mean we should ignore legitimate food safety concerns, but rather that we should place them in proper perspective.**

He considers anxiety over diet far more potentially damaging to most people's health than GMOs, salmonella, pesticides, or any other of the food scares many people fret over. He counsels a simple, balanced diet as the best choice.

Labeling: For or Against?

Labeling foods such as produce turns out to be a complex issue. It is not just a question of yes or no—should the government require produce to be labeled or not? It is also a question of what kind of labeling should be done, what kinds of standards should be set, and how the labeling regulations will be enforced. Arguments on all sides tend to be both passionate and persuasive since the topic under discussion has to do with the food we eat and what we need to know about it. In the case of farmers and researchers, we are also talking about their livelihood and their professions.

Pluses

- Consumer advocacy groups make the point that people need to know the ingredients in what they eat, how their food was produced or raised, and other factors relevant to safety and nutrition. They assert that only then can people buying their family's food make informed, intelligent food purchases. Many consumers agree—especially those who can afford higher costs in foods.

- People with allergies to petrochemicals and special sensitivities have a need for labels containing information about whether pesticides were used, the presence of ingredients they might be allergic to (such as peanuts), and other information that can help them avoid unpleasant or even life-threatening reactions.

- Dietitians, nutritionists, nurses, and other health professionals usually favor labeling, especially when it

includes information on factors such as nutrients, calo-
ries, and additives that may affect the health and well-
being of their clients.

Minuses

• Farmers, growers, and food manufacturers who are
required to supply labeling for their produce or food
products may object to the increased costs of collecting
the information and supplying printed labels.

• Libertarians and others who promote the cause of
individual freedom and laissez-faire government often
object to the added bureaucratic level required to en-
force labeling regulations, as well as the interference
by government in an area of commerce that they feel
would be better managed by market pressures.

• Consumers who are unable to afford or unwilling to
pay the increased costs of food labeling (since raised
prices are inevitable) tend to be against labeling. The
U.S. Department of Agriculture side-stepped this
objection somewhat by requiring labeling only from
producers who claim to offer organic foods. Thus,
those who want organic foods will pay a slightly
higher premium, but those who can't afford the extra
cost or don't care whether what they eat is organic remain relatively unaffected. Producers of GMO-free foods
can label them as such, while those who sell GM foods only
have to label them if a potential allergen is present;
for example, "Do not eat if allergic to nuts."

4
Improving on Nature's Forests

THE TEST TUBE FOREST

Business, February 2002

Consider the spreading chestnut tree—all but disappeared from the Atlantic coastal states to which it was once native. The chestnut succumbed in the early 1900s to an accidentally imported fungus, and almost none of these trees are alive today, although they once dominated forests from Maine to Georgia and west to the Mississippi River.

Tree experts could breed the chestnut with Asian trees that are similar but not susceptible to the fungus. However, that would take several human generations. A quicker method might be to use genetic modification techniques to insert the protective genes from the Asian trees into some of the few existing chestnut trees, creating a resistant chestnut.

Other ideas abound for modifying trees. The first genetically modified (GM) trees were created in the late 1980s, and by 1998 a tree that made better paper was designed by a team of researchers at Michigan Technological University. Traditional paper manufacture begins with cut lumber, which is debarked, chipped, treated, and reduced to a pulp which ultimately is pressed into sheets of paper. Lignin is a natural adhesive that binds the cellulose fibers of wood together. To convert wood chips into pulp, the fibers have to be broken down through the use of chemicals, so the less lignin there is in the wood, the easier and faster the process. Also, the more cellulose there is, the stronger the paper. Researcher Vincent Chiang, who led the group, called for modifying aspen trees by inserting genes that reduced the lignin content by half. They also stepped up the quantity of cellulose as much as 15 percent, strengthening the paper. With these two genetic changes they grew a tree that required less processing and produced stronger paper, thereby decreasing the cost of making paper. As of April 2002, these aspen trees had begun field trials. So the GM timber boom may already have begun.

Making Better Lumber

The timber industry has always been key to the health of the economy in North America, but many conservationists have become concerned about clear-cutting practices and the huge reduction in forests in the last century. Lumber companies have sometimes exhausted their own natural resource. The solution of genetically modified (GM) trees looks so promising to several large paper companies

The Connection: Paper and Bioengineered Trees

What is the connection between trees and paper? First manufactured by Chinese inventors more than 2,000 years ago, paper has a long history. For many centuries, manufacturers made paper out of hemp, flax, and later, cotton fiber. (Even today, the finest paper has a high "rag" content, indicating the percentage of cotton fiber used.) However, the many uses for paper caused a demand that exceeded these resources. Meanwhile, in the early 1700s, French scientist René de Réaumur observed that the papery substance from which wasps make their nests is actually made of wood fiber. (The wasps would chew up the wood and then spit it out when it was mushy.) These fibers, the primary component of wood, are made of cellulose. They are the backbone of a tree's cell walls and in nature they are tightly stuck together by an adhesive substance called lignin, allowing the tree to gain strength and height. The challenge was to free the cellulose fibers from the lignin, a complex material that is not easily biodegradable.

In the early 1840s, German inventor Friedrich Keller came up with the idea of pressing wood against a wet grinding wheel to separate the fibers, resulting in the first wood pulp. From that, he saw that a strong, smooth paper could be made.

Today, most of the fiber supply for making paper comes from recycled paper, cardboard, and sawmill by-products, such as chips, sawdust, and shavings. Very little comes directly from logs harvested from forests. However, ultimately, all these products come from trees.

THE TIMBER INDUSTRY IS STARTING TO USE GENETIC ENGINEERING TO KEEP FROM EXHAUSTING ITS OWN NATURAL RESOURCE—TREES. IN THIS INSTANCE, BARK IS BEING GRAFTED ONTO ANOTHER TREE TO PRODUCE CRISPER APPLES. ENVIRONMENTALISTS DO NOT THINK THAT GRAFTING IS A GOOD SOLUTION.

that they have joined together in an enterprise called ArborGen, a $60-million venture dedicated to developing transgenic trees for lumber. The development could reduce the impact made by these interests on U.S. land use and forests.

Bt toxin could also be introduced genetically, as has been done in corn, cotton, potatoes, and other plants. This would reduce the tree's susceptibility to pests.

In Victoria, British Columbia, another group named CellFor is working on the Douglas fir, a tall, straight-trunked tree—excellent for lumber. These natural giants in the world of trees take many years to grow, however, so researchers are looking for ways to find a shortcut. They are working on techniques for mass-replicating exact copies of some of the best specimens of this superb timber tree. Their straight 200-foot-tall trunks are strong and free from knots, and the trees developed by CellFor grow rapidly.

Because CellFor has been accused of creating "Frankenforests," CellFor keeps a low profile. The company has no sign on its office door, and its phone number is unlisted. The researchers say similar labs have sometimes been fire-bombed by outraged activists. Environmentalists are understandably worried, even though fire-bombing is a reprehensibly dangerous and violent way to express their concern. They are upset because tree pollen can travel vast distances and pollinate non-GM trees. GM seeds can be carried miles away by the winds, and the environmental havoc caused by mixing GM trees and non-GM trees could be substantial. These are issues that will have to be resolved before going forward with the superforests these research teams envision.

Is It in the Wind?

The wind may be one of nature's most efficient tools for seed dispersal, but it's the genetic engineer's greatest foe when it comes to plants. Pollen from a genetically modified crop can literally sail on the winds into another farmer's field and contaminate the non-GM crops that grow there. Depending on the changes made in the GM crop, such an outcome could range from mildly undesirable to disastrous. What if a GM crop cross-pollinates with a non-GM food crop and the resulting produce gets shipped to market? No one knows these genetically modified organisms (GMOs) are present. Consumers eat the food made from the crop, allergic reactions could occur, and people could get sick or die. Or maybe that disastrous scenario would not occur. What are the real risks?

Other, less disastrous risks also exist. In the case of Bt corn, for example, inspectors check for evidence of GM crops among those that are certified not to be GM. If GMOs are found, the shipment is refused, and the farmer makes no money on that shipment of produce. This can amount to a big loss for the innocent farmer who had the bad luck to have a field adjacent to a GM crop.

Risk and consequences are difficult to evaluate in advance. Some environmental groups—including the international activist group known as Greenpeace—therefore advise a policy known as the "Precautionary Principle."

Basically, this principle suggests a policy that is meant to protect the environment and calls for taking preventive action at the source of a potential problem before damage has begun to occur. In its strictest application supporters point out that many mistakes have irreversible consequences, so the burden of proof must rest on proving that the procedure is safe. And if no proof of harm may ever be possible—without causing irreversible damage—people should not be allowed to try things out to see what would happen. Greenpeace rightly points out that both human health and the environment have been damaged by human carelessness, so their Precautionary Principle requires enacting a policy that calls for zero risk. The principle holds that any activity must be halted for which the risk is greater than zero. The European Environmental Bureau (EEB) has adopted a slightly modified Precautionary Principle for the member countries of the European Union (EU).

Many policymakers think the Precautionary Principle is too broad and inhibiting. Careful risk management, in this alternative opinion, must be used and progress needs to proceed with caution, but zero risk is often impossible. Most human technological advances, including the use of electricity, would not be available to us today if our ancestors had invoked the Precautionary Principle.

Is compromise possible between these two opposing viewpoints? Resolving questions of acceptable levels of risk to both humans and the environment remain among the most important issues to be resolved in the field of genetic engineering.

GM Forests: For or Against?

Is genetic engineering among non-food plants such as trees a good idea? What are the pros and cons of biotech forestry?

Pluses

• Without biotechnology, we may never be able to recover the chestnut tree and other threatened species of trees and other plants. Other trees and plants might well be improved or serve to help produce beneficial products.

• Genetic engineering can help reduce the cost and increase the strength of paper by lowering the lignin levels on wood and increasing the cellulose levels in wood. By cloning the Douglas fir, researchers can make the big tree's strong, straight-grain wood more widely available. Similar advantages are sure to be offered by the use of biotechnology with other types of trees.

Minuses

* Environmentalists are concerned about contamination when seeds travel outside the research area. This is a broad concern that applies to crops as well as trees, and even some biotech animals, such as fish, which could also easily slip out of control. Intermingling of GMOs with organisms that occur naturally could affect the biodiversity of our planet and endanger natural species—threatening the integrity of the planet's ecosystem. The warning is a serious one. According to biologist Jean Emberlin of Britain's National

Pollen Research Unit and University College, Worcester, "Once the pollen is out there it is very difficult to redress the situation. I don't think it would be wise to go ahead without knowing more about the possible repercussions."

• Farmers likewise are concerned about contamination—since long years of managing their planting and harvests of a particular strain of crop, such as hard red spring wheat, can be ruined by pollen on the blowing wind from a neighboring GM field.

5
Cloning Animals: New, Yet Old

EWE AGAIN? CLONING FROM ADULT DNA

Science News online, March 1, 1997

On May 2, 2002, Cynthia Batchelder was among the happiest of graduate students. On that day, a calf named Rosie was born. Of course, Rosie was not just any calf—she was a clone, the second born on the University of California at Davis campus, but the first to live more than three days. Batchelder, a doctoral student in animal science, who led the team in the cattle cloning project, said at the press conference less than a week after the birth: "[Rosie is] so healthy and aggressive right now, which is just great."

Rosie was delivered by Caesarean section. Her weight at birth was a little high but within normal limits. Within six days, Batchelder reported, "She follows me around the pen; she loves to have her chin tickled."

Dolly's Legacy

Five years after the birth of Dolly in Scotland, the birth of Rosie the calf was not front-page news. Plenty of other animals had already been cloned. Successful genetic copies had been made of other sheep, as well as mice, goats, pigs, rabbits, cattle, and even a cat. A small herd of cloned cows already exists in the United States, and some genetic engineering advocates think all of our beef will soon come from cloned cattle.

The team cloning Rosie used much the same technique as was used for cloning Dolly. In a process known as *gene transfer*, a cell nucleus—with its supply of DNA—was removed from an (over age fourteen) Hereford cow (a type of reddish-brown and white beef cattle from England) and placed into the nucleus of an unfertilized raw egg. Then a zap of electricity encouraged the egg to begin dividing. After seven days, the growing embryo was placed in the uterus of a Hereford-Angus crossbred cow called a black baldy. Rosie, though, is a purebred Hereford, like her genetic mother, with a white face and a reddish-brown body.

Researcher Cynthia Batchelder did not just wave her magic wand, mutter some special words, and produce a perfect clone the first time she tried. The technique may be five years old, but it still has a few glitches. Batchelder produced about 900 embryos in 18 months. Only 87 of those survived long enough to be placed in a cow's uterus. Very few—only 13 or 14—lived long enough to attach to the uterus wall of the surrogate mother and began to develop. Most of those miscarried early in the first trimester. (Cows have a nine-month pregnancy, the same length as humans.) Batchelder's research centers on a comparison of how well different types of cells do at producing cattle clones (which may help explain the many failures). Rosie began as a granulosa cell,

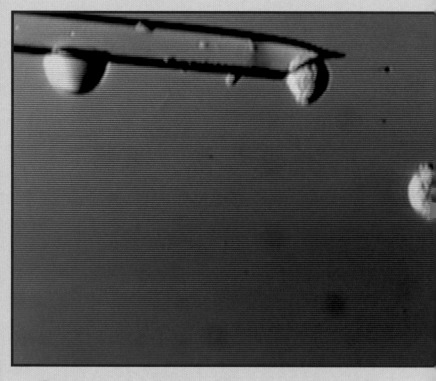

CLONING BEGINS IN A WORLD SO SMALL THAT IT CAN ONLY BE VIEWED THROUGH EXTREME MAGNIFICATION. THIS IMAGE IS A LIGHT MICROGRAPH OF A MICRONEEDLE SUCKING UP AN EMBRYONIC SHEEP CELL AS THE FIRST STEP IN CLONING A SHEEP.

Microsopic Genetically Modified Do-Gooders

Most people know that insulin saves lives. Insulin, a natural hormone provided by the human pancreas, regulates the metabolism of carbohydrates and fats and converts glucose to glycogen, necessary for a person's energy needs. A serious and widespread chronic illness known as diabetes mellitus (type I) occurs when a person's pancreas cannot produce natural insulin. Serious symptoms can result, including poor circulation, gangrene, and even death. Scientists found that diabetes can be treated through injections of insulin, but insulin is often in short supply and expensive.

That's where genetic engineering came into the picture. As mentioned earlier, by altering genes in certain bacteria, scientists turned these tiny organisms into microscopic drug-making factories. In the early 1980s, using genetic engineering techniques, the human gene that carried the recipe for making insulin was inserted into a bacterium by scientists at Genentech. Because DNA is a language understood by all living things, the transfer resulted in production of human insulin. Everyone diagnosed with this type of diabetes has been taking insulin produced in this way ever since. Insulin is much more readily available and producing it no longer requires the use of pigs, sheep, and cattle. It is also a perfect fit because it is human, as we are. Best of all, it has saved countless lives.

which is a cell found in the ovaries. As of May 2002, only two of Batchelder's embryos had reached birth.

If cloning is so difficult, why pursue it? Because researchers believe it could end up making a big difference in food production, once they learn how to succeed more consistently. Just as ranchers and farmers have tried to breed desirable traits into their herds for thousands of years, now genetic engineering experts have begun introducing genes from other species through cloning to produce livestock that grow faster and bigger. They can also be designed to produce lower-cholesterol meat. Ranchers constantly seek to breed longer-lived cows that produce strong calves and have higher quality meat.

Scientists have been working on this project since the 1980s and have split and re-split a set of embryos, producing a total of 1,400 cows.

Saving the Endangered

If a species is dying out, cloning could provide the key to preventing its extinction. In October 2001, the first report came out that a successful clone of a member of an endangered species had been accomplished. Thanks to the efforts of a team led by Pasqualino Loi at the University of Teramo in Italy, the world's smallest wild sheep received a new lease on life. The news, published in *Nature Biotechnology*, involves a "toy" sheep known as the mouflon and found on the islands of Corsica, Sardinia, and Cyprus, off the coast of Italy. Scientists think it comes from an ancient line and is a close relative of the Asian mouflon, believed to be the ancestor of all domestic sheep.

The disappearing mouflon thrived on its rocky isles until about 1850, when hunters depleted its numbers dangerously. Rescuers transported most remaining mouflons to other parts of Europe, where thousands of them live today. However, they are dangerously scarce in their native habitat.

For conservationists, Dolly's successful creation prompted a debate over the merits and drawbacks of using biotechnology to rescue endangered species. Loi and his colleagues think that by collecting cell samples from endangered species before their numbers dwindle too dangerously, a cell bank could be formed that would ensure the continuation of the species beyond its natural limits.

Other conservationists are concerned that people will fall back on this fragile crutch instead of making sure that the numbers of endangered species do not become dangerously low. They believe that the habitat needs to be protected and poaching and other threats need to be eliminated or reduced. If these things are taken care of, then numbers will climb again.

However, in the opinion of Betsy Dresser, who directs the Audubon Center for Research of Endangered Species in New Orleans, Louisiana, protecting the habitat could easily fall short of the goal of protecting the species from extinction. She points out, "Any tool for saving endangered species is important. Cloning is just another reproductive tool, like in-vitro fertilization."

The cloned mouflon lamb had a background similar to Dolly's. Adult cells were used in the process known as somatic cell nuclear transfer. But the mouflon lamb's surrogate mother was a different species—an ordinary domestic sheep. She provided the unfertilized egg that received a transplanted nucleus from somatic cells of a mouflon. She also successfully carried the clone until it was ready for birth.

Renewing the Gene Pool

Geneticist Oliver Ryder, from the Center for Reproduction of Endangered Species at the San Diego Zoo in California, agrees with Pasqualino Loi, who cloned the mouflon lamb. Ryder says that cloning can be used to bring back "a significant

Why Biodiversity?

What is biodiversity, and why are conservationists so concerned about protecting endangered species? When talking about plants and animals, the term "endangered" means they are in danger of becoming extinct. Once the last individuals of a species die off, they are gone forever. Thousands of species have been designated as endangered. Some endangered animals include ocelots, Tasmanian forester kangaroos, bighorn sheep, some species of falcons, salamanders, whales, crocodiles, and egrets, to name just a few. Others, such as the bald eagle, remain on a list of threatened species—those that are likely to become endangered if they are not protected.

The U.S. Congress passed the Endangered Species Act in 1973 to protect the habitat of any rare, threatened, and endangered species. The International Union for the Conservation of Nature (IUCN) in Switzerland represents groups in about 140 countries. Their common goal is to maintain "biodiversity"—a shorthand term that stands for biological diversity, or the many different species of living things. Why worry about biodiversity? Most conservationists see diversity of the species as necessary to our continued well-being and the health of our planet. They cite ecological, ethical, aesthetic, and cultural reasons, as well as economic justifications for their concerns:

• **Ecosystem processes. The processes that support life on our planet rely on complex interdependencies between species of living things and their habitats (ecosystems). Conservationists point out that if we destroy portions of these ecosystems then all life everywhere will suffer.**

• **Ethics. Squandering Earth's resources results in short-changing the potential of other species as well as future generations of humans on our planet.**

• **Aesthetics and culture. The beauty of the environment and the wealth of biological diversity contribute to cultures and aesthetic values all over the world.**

• **Economics. Living things contribute to economic health in many ways, supplying food, medicines, energy and building materials.**

AT ORIGEN THERAPEUTICS, A BIOTECHNOLOGY FIRM IN BURLINGAME, CALIFORNIA, RESEARCHERS ARE TESTING PROCESSES FOR USING NUCLEAR TRANSFER TO PRODUCE A TRANSGENIC CHICKEN DESIGNED TO BE MEATIER.

slice of the gene pool pie" that has been lost. Reintroduction could be carefully managed in zoos and controlled circumstances, and many naturally evolved species could be saved that have been destroyed by overhunting, pesticide side effects, infertility, or other factors. By this means, humans might be able to undo some of the harm they have already done.

Effects on Foods?

What about the milk and meat that come from cloned cows and other livestock? Are they safe? Some consumers worry that unnatural effects will result from eating meat or drinking milk from cows that genetic engineers have tampered with. However, milk and meat from cloned cows have already entered the marketplace.

Animal science professor Joy Mench of the University of California at Davis points out that the 1,400 cloned animals produced from embryo splits are no different than twins. So, if the milk from the original animal is safe, the milk from the rest should be equally safe.

What about Protecting Nature?

Some scientists worry that genetically altered fish, insects, and birds may mingle with natural wildlife species and cause ecological havoc. Domestic animals, such as cows and other livestock, are not airborne or waterborne and are unlikely to affect wildlife by breeding with wild species. A National Academy of Sciences (NAS) panel, reporting at the request of the U.S. Food and Drug Administration (FDA), announced in August 2002 that they were less concerned about the effects of genetic engineering on the food and milk provided by GM cows than the effect of GM birds and fish on the natural environment.

A company in Massachusetts has engineered a fast-growing salmon. Another company has developed an insect that feeds on insect pests but, unlike the pests it destroys, is unaffected by pesticides. Both of these new products could easily escape into the environment and cause problems if they got out of control.

For example, if a transgenic fast-growing salmon escaped into the wild, it could out-compete the natural species for food and other resources. Conservationists fear that the fast-growing salmon might become more successful competitors for the food supply and for mates than their natural counterparts in the wild. As one critic remarked, "Once you get the genie out of the bottle, you can't put it back again."

Selling only sterile transgenic female fish might solve the problem, but no one really knows.

Solutions, Anyone?

Animal biotechnology holds some exciting possibilities, but, as the NAS panel noted, no single U.S. government agency is charged with monitoring this infant industry. The FDA, the Environmental Protection Agency (EPA), and the U.S. Department of Agriculture (USDA) all have jurisdiction over parts of the industry, but there are some gaps and overlaps in their combined oversight. The result is confusion and disarray in terms of coordinated regulation. What the situation calls for, according to the NAS scientists, is an increase in integrated monitoring and a more realistic evaluation of the risks of animal biotechnology.

Morality and Animal Cloning

However, a significant segment of the population finds these arguments insignificant in the face of what they see as a larger issue: the morality of cloning plants and animals. In a survey conducted in 1992 by sociologist Thomas Hoban, about 26 percent of the American public felt that genetically engineering plants was morally wrong. About twice that many—53 percent—felt that using genetic engineering on animals was morally wrong. The unsurprising conclusion he reached was that more Americans saw a problem with animals than with plants. Though this study is a decade old, Hoban supposes people still think the same way.

Hoban's study did not explore *why* respondents felt the way they did. Dan Charles, a commentator for *Morn-*

ing Edition (a radio program on National Public Radio), summed up Hoban's current thoughts in a program that aired August 21, 2002:

> **We humans care more about animals than we do about plants, Hoban says. They're closer to us. Whatever scientists do to a cow, we can imagine them doing to us. Hoban has been a consultant to biotech companies, and he has supported genetically engineered crops. But he is not so sure about animal biotech. And most of the companies currently involved in animal biotechnology, he says, don't seem to realize they're wandering into a minefield of emotion.**

Animal welfare advocates are concerned about problems that have occurred with cloned animals that were born malformed or with defects, experienced a difficult delivery, or died at an early age. These problems happen more frequently with animals cloned in the way Dolly was—from somatic cells instead of stem cells. Dolly was a huge success and gained enormous publicity. However, the story of the second ewe, born shortly after Dolly, was sadder. From birth, she panted constantly. Otherwise she seemed fine, but her breathing was so labored that the researchers became worried about her quality of life. The respiratory problem did not clear up, so after a few weeks the team decided to euthanize her. An autopsy revealed that the animal's lungs were not properly developed. Animal rights activists are concerned about the ethics of human treatment of animals. They generally oppose mistreatment of animals, scientific experimentation on animals, and hunting, especially for sport. Some animal rights adherents take a more extreme position than others do, but most are alarmed at placing animals at risk for suffering and object to cloning animals.

Others object, not in defense of a political cause, but because the process is unnatural. This is a wide-ranging psychological and emotional issue having many roots.

For some people, the issue is religious or philosophical—humans, they believe, should not tamper with the creations of nature or God. They see human technology as interfering with natural processes. Some sects, such as the Mennonites, reject nearly all recent technological advances. They continue to live in a manner more common to the nineteenth century—a lifestyle that embraces wheeled carts, harnesses, and horse-drawn plows, but not the machinery of the industrial age or the electronic devices of the twenty-first century.

Most people prefer to embrace the many conveniences offered by technology. Supermarket clerks, real estate agents, grandparents, kids, and company presidents all make use of cell phones, computers, DVD players, and microwave ovens. Yet, many of these people have a moral problem with genetic engineering. How do they decide where to draw the line? Some, as Thomas Hoban pointed out, stop at genetically engineered animals. For them, the question of genetically engineered plants may not seem very different from the common practice of gassing tomatoes with ethylene or thousands of other changes typically made in produce. However, most people are aware of consciousness in mammals, reptiles, fish, and many other animals. Consciousness makes them seem different—closer by far to human beings. People identify much more closely with animals, and interfering with natural animal processes can therefore seem morally wrong—especially since animals have no choice or say in the matter. In an effort to avoid exploiting animals, some people do not eat meat. Others extend their commitment by not eating animal products such as eggs or even cheese. And some do not wear or use leather, which is made from animal hides.

This line of reasoning has a consistent logic. But a lot of people who recoil at genetically engineered animals have no problem with drinking milk, wearing leather, and eating meat, eggs, and cheese. For them, the issue may be simply a matter of tradition.

Animal Cloning: For or Against?

The birth of Dolly was for many people an exciting, even if anxiety-producing, breakthrough in science. But her death at age six, at about half her breed's life expectancy, caused many people to pause and ask if cloning is really as safe as Dolly initially had made it look.

Pluses

• **Genetic engineering and cloning can be used to revive endangered species such as the mouflon sheep.**

• **GM or cloned animals can be "programmed" to develop rapidly, putting food on the table more quickly. They can also be bred with greater nutritional value than conventional meats.**

• **Cloned animals can help scientists gain understanding about genetic engineering, organisms, and biology at this highly complex level.**

Minuses

• Many people question the safety of food derived from GM cows, goats, and other animals. Is the inexpensive GM cheese that is available in New Zealand as safe as tests seem to indicate? How safe is milk from GM cows? What about GM meat?

• The early death of Dolly has raised concerns about potential human clones as well. According to ethicist Patrick Dixon, "The greatest worry many scientists have is that human clones—even if they don't have monstrous abnormalities in the womb—will need hip replacements in their teenage years and perhaps develop senile dementia by their twentieth birthday."

• Animal rights activists have similar concerns for the animals themselves—who may suffer a range of risks not faced by non-GE animals, including shortened life spans and abnormal susceptibility to ailments and birth defects.

• Some GM animals, such as fish and birds, are at risk of escaping into the natural environment, throwing off the natural environmental balance, pushing native species to extinction, and wreaking havoc with diversity as we know it today.

6
The Human Genome: Research Breakthrough

"BUBBLE BOY" GENE THERAPY HALTED

Experimental treatment tied to possible leukemia side effect

MSNBC News, October 3, 2002

Rhys Evans was born with a rare problem, sometimes called the "bubble boy" condition—which prevented him from developing an immune system. Without any way to ward off infection, he had to be carefully isolated in a sterile environment. He spent most of his first eighteen months of life in a hospital instead of at his home in Treharris near Cardiff, Wales, in the United Kingdom (U.K.).

Today, Rhys is cured. He plays happily outside like any normal boy.

Rhys's problem is called severe combined immunodeficiency (SCID), and it is caused by the mutation of a single

AFFLICTED WITH SEVERE COMBINED IMMUNE DEFICIENCY, THIS BOY
LIVED IN A PLASTIC ENCLOSED ENVIRONMENT—DUBBED "THE BUBBLE"
BY THE MEDIA. DAVID VETTER DIED IN 1984 AT THE AGE OF TWELVE,
BUT, AS PICTURED HERE IN 1980, HE LIVED A LIFE FILLED WITH AS MUCH
FUN AS HE COULD PACK IN. TODAY, SOME RESEARCHERS HOPE THAT
GENE THERAPY MAY HELP "BUBBLE BOYS" LIKE DAVID, BUT AS OF 2003,
THE PATH REMAINS CONTROVERSIAL AND UNCERTAIN.

gene. Doctors at Great Ormond Street Hospital in London tried a breakthrough treatment—by replacing the culprit gene with a duplicate that was not mutated. The result was announced in April 2002—an exciting moment both for his doctors and for Rhys and his family.

However, another boy was not so lucky. After three years of gene therapy begun just after his birth, he seemed to be responding very well. In the spring of 2002, he even recovered from an infection that would have threatened his life without the gene replacement. Then the summer months brought bad news: an overproduction of white blood cells that produced symptoms similar to leukemia. Even though several other children with SCID—including nine in Paris—seemed to be doing well with the therapy, scientists working on the project in both France and the United States called a halt to the trials in October 2002. Some were already in progress; others were about to begin.

But the children's physicians concluded that the risk was too great to continue without further research and precautions in place. For the families, hope has been put on hold.

Genetically modified (GM) foods have stirred up controversy. Some people are uneasy about animal cloning. However, when it comes to genetic engineering and humans, many people instantly imagine a mad scientist who oversteps human bounds and takes on the role of a god. Gene therapy, stem cell research, and human cloning awaken visions of Frankenstein's monster. Yet eighteen-month-old Rhys Evans is a charming little red-headed boy who likes trains. What could be more normal?

Biotechnology has provided powerful tools for medicine. Yet, in this field perhaps more than any other, scientists have to proceed with great caution. Ethics—the process of determining right and wrong—has always held a key position in medical research and practice. And now the growing field of medical biotechnology has added many new ethical issues, resulting in a field known as bioethics.

Scientists find themselves facing many difficult decisions, and the benefits and risks of biotechnology must be weighed carefully.

The Human Genome

In 1990, teams of scientists worldwide began a coordinated effort to map the human genome—the full set of human genes. On June 26, 2000, the international project came to an important milestone: The first map of some 30,000 genes was completed. That day, U.S. president Bill Clinton made the announcement, with U.K. prime minister Tony Blair at his side. This important breakthrough, he said, would lead to new ways to prevent, diagnose, treat, and cure disease. Scientists estimate that unwanted mutations in people's genes are responsible for some 5,000 diseases that clearly have hereditary causes. Examples range from Huntington's disease to cystic fibrosis and sickle cell anemia. Genetics also affect the development of many thousands of other diseases.

International partners, including China, France, Germany, Japan, and the United Kingdom, joined the United States in funding and pursuing this giant breakthrough project. The process of connecting a gene with an inherited disease used to take years. Now the process is complete in a matter of days. In 1997, thanks to the Human Genome Project, scientists took only nine days to map a gene for Parkinson's disease.

With the working draft of the human genome completed, scientists could make use of the information already

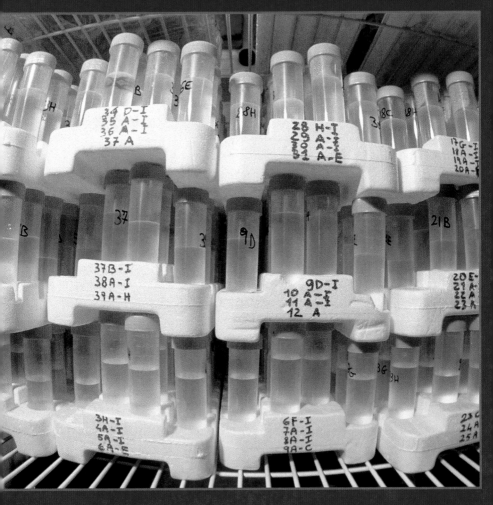

HUMAN GENE BANK: THIS LABORATORY REFRIGERATOR IS STOCKED WITH TEST TUBES CONTAINING THE ENTIRE HUMAN GENOME. EACH TUBE CONTAINS A PARTICULAR REGION OF THE **DNA** FOUND ON ANY ONE OF THE FORTY-SIX CHROMOSOMES FROM A HUMAN CELL. CLONED AND STORED FRAGMENTS LIKE THESE MADE UP MANY OF THE GENE BANKS COMMONLY USED DURING THE **HUMAN GENOME PROJECT.**

found in several ways. The White House press release named several approaches to inherited disease that would soon be possible. Physicians would soon be able to:

• **Let patients know when they are at risk for certain diseases. After scientists have found out which changes in a gene's DNA sequence can cause disease, physicians can test healthy patients to find out whether their gene structure may put them at risk later in life for genetically tied ailments such as diabetes or prostate cancer. Patients and their physicians can use this awareness of risk to take precautions. A preventive prescription, changes in diet, exercise, and other changes in lifestyle may serve to prevent the disease, and a screening program may catch it early enough for treatment.**

• **Diagnose disease more precisely and choose the most effective treatment. By using genetic analysis, physicians can break diseases down into more closely defined categories—for example, into types of colon cancer and skin cancer. Armed with more precise classifications, scientists can use a patient's genetic fingerprint to design drugs for that individual's predicted response. This approach would be especially effective in designing a chemotherapy treatment plan for a cancer patient. Using a genetic fingerprint of the patient's tumor, specialists can choose the types of chemotherapy that are most likely to be effective.**

• **Predict the course of disease more accurately. More precise diagnosis will also help doctors know how fast a disease may progress. This information**

Using Genome Knowledge

The uses of genetic knowledge in human medicine take many forms. Sometimes, instead of replacing an entire gene, just replacing the protein product of the defective gene may prove both more effective and easier. Or, instead, clinicians may introduce a small molecule chosen for the way it can interact with the protein to change its behavior.

Researchers had good success with this approach when they developed a drug to treat chronic myelogenous leukemia (CML). This form of leukemia results from the uncontrolled growth of white blood cells. A type of cancer, the disease may be present for several years with only minor symptoms. Eventually, though, the stem cells in the bone marrow produce vast numbers of leukemic cells (cancerous white blood cells), and the patient enters a potentially life-threatening crisis. The molecular treatment targets the genetic flaw causing the disease, attaching to the abnormal protein caused by the genetic flaw and blocking its activity. In preliminary tests reported as of June 2000, blood counts returned to normal in all patients treated with the drug. Another study showed that nearly 90 percent of CML patients treated with this special molecule showed no further progression of their disease. The drug, STI571 (Gleevec), was approved in 2001 by the FDA for patients in all phases of CML.

Gleevec works on the product of the CML cells, and not on the cells themselves or their genetics, so technically it is not genetic engineering. It is, however, a stunning example of the progress to be gained through an understanding of the human genome and how it works. In the words of Dr. Richard Klausner, former director of the National Cancer Institute, "For the first time, cancer researchers [now] have the necessary tools to probe the molecular anatomy of tumor cells in search of cancer-causing proteins. "Gleevec offers proof that molecular targeting works in treating cancer, provided that the target is correctly chosen. The challenge now is to find these targets."

can help with decisions about the risks and benefits of treatments.

* **Develop new, molecular-level treatments. Better treatments can result from the molecular view scientists are now gaining. Completion of the human genome helps researchers understand how genes work and what processes at the molecular level are causing disease. This knowledge can make a dramatic difference in the area of drug design for curing genetically caused diseases.**

Promise and Challenge

As the Human Genome Project rolls toward completion in 2003, government, scientists, physicians, and the public alike have developed a heightened understanding of the many implications—both promising and challenging—its completion entails. The work carries with it many social, ethical, and legal ramifications. These challenges touch many aspects of the biotechnology industry, but nowhere have they stirred up more controversy than in the applications of genetic engineering to human subjects.

The Human Stem Cell Controversy

ACTOR CHRISTOPHER REEVE MAKES HIS CASE FOR STEM CELL RESEARCH

NewsFactor Network, October 4, 2002

FORCING TAXPAYERS TO FUND DESTRUCTION OF EMBRYOS "ILLEGAL, IMMORAL AND UNNECESSARY," CATHOLIC OFFICIAL SAYS

United States Conference of Catholic Bishops Communications, July 18, 2001

Stem cells are the undifferentiated cells that have multiple possibilities for development, which is why they are so useful for therapeutic applications. The problem is that embryos are used in most human stem cell research. Even though the embryos are very early-stage embryos—about the size of a period at the end of a sentence—some bioethicists consider even such an early-stage embryo to be a human life.

Large ethical, moral, and legal questions therefore surround stem cell research (derived from embryos), also known as therapeutic cloning (as opposed to reproductive cloning, discussed in the next chapter). President George W. Bush opposes both types of biotechnology and, as of early 2003, many decisions about the future of these two applications of genetic engineering hung in the balance. Even after decisions are made and legislation passed, the debate will continue.

What Is Therapeutic Cloning?

Therapeutic cloning is not the same process that brought us Dolly. It involves removing the nucleus of an unfertilized egg cell, replacing it with the material from the nucleus of a differentiated cell (also known as a somatic cell, such as a nerve cell, skin cell, or heart cell). Then, researchers use electricity or some other stimulation to prod the cell to start dividing. Stem cells are formed after the cell begins dividing, within five to six days. Then researchers can extract the stem cells and begin using them for study and therapeutic medicine—often referred to as stem cell research.

Through therapeutic cloning researchers hope to be able to cure many destructive diseases for which there is currently no effective treatment. Tissue and cells damaged by disease might be mended through the use of cloned replacement cells and tissue, restoring function to organs and saving lives. Basic research on the development of stem cells can help scientists step up their search for new treatments and cures, tailor treatments to individuals, and develop stem cells that resist attack and destruction by the body's immune system—an especially promising prospect for patients who have diabetes, heart disease, or spinal cord injuries.

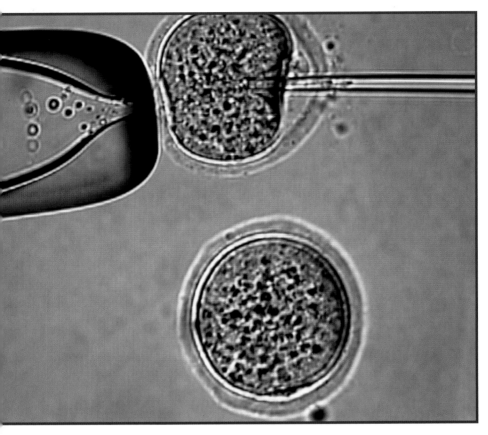

STEM CELL RESEARCH: IN THIS LIGHT MICROGRAPH, A NEEDLE (UPPER RIGHT)
IS BEING USED TO INJECT ADULT GENETIC MATERIAL INTO A MOUSE EGG
(UPPER CENTER) FROM WHICH THE ORIGINAL GENETIC MATERIAL HAS BEEN
EMPTIED. FROM THIS MATERIAL, EMBRYONIC STEM CELLS WILL DEVELOP, THE
FIRST STEP IN THE DEVELOPMENT OF AN EMBRYO. FROM THESE STEM CELLS,
ALL THE SPECIALIZED CELLS OF THE ORGANISM FORM.

The Ethics of Using Embryonic Stem Cells

Part of the controversy over this kind of research centers on the question of whether existing stem cell lines are sufficient for the research that needs to be done. Currently, only existing cell lines are approved for use. Therapeutic cloning advocates say that this is not enough. The Bush administration is sure that existing stocks are adequate, and since these existing cell lines would never develop into human lives anyway, the issue of killing an embryo is moot—or at least, less important. But American researchers have access to only a limited number of stem cell lines—not enough to proceed with aggressive investigation of treatments and cures.

However, researchers also contend that therapeutic cloning sidesteps the ethical issue because fertilization of the egg by a sperm, implantation in the uterus, or pregnancy does not take place. They draw a distinction between cloning with the intent of making a human being and cloning to make research possible for understanding and treating terrible diseases.

Adult stem cell research could provide an alternative, and it would be less objectionable, since using adult cells would not require destroying an embryo. However, scientists at both the National Institutes of Health (NIH) and the National Academy of Sciences (NAS) agree that embryonic stem cells are ideal for research because these cells can make any cell in the body. They also can be grown in a lab indefinitely. Adult cells do not have these advantages.

Another area of concern is the potential for exploitation of women to obtain eggs for research. Would therapeutic cloning lead to a market for women's eggs? Advocates meet this concern by explaining that therapeutic cloning would not produce a market for eggs. The first purpose of therapeutic cloning is to perform research in order to understand how cells develop. Once this is understood, researchers can replicate the process in a laboratory and the need for new eggs will end. Legislation should supply safeguards and ethical standards protecting women, providing for informed consent, and preventing undue financial inducements.

Unlimited Stem Cell Research, Moratorium, or Ban?

Questions about the bioethics inherent in therapeutic cloning have caused the U.S. government and other concerned citizens to be hesitant about allowing unlimited stem cell research and therapeutic cloning. They have proposed several other solutions to the dilemmas posed by these lines of research. One is the idea of a moratorium on further therapeutic cloning. This idea may sound less final and less devastating to future research than a ban. However, in some ways it is worse. In fact, researchers say, a moratorium would bring productive research to a grinding halt and, once imposed, would be difficult to undo.

Most scientists would have to abandon stem cell research. They would find funding difficult or impossible to obtain and any further research they attempted to do would be frowned on. Their talents would be lost to the profession in this field. Once turned to other lines of research, the career paths of these scientists would be set and attracting good researchers back into the field would be difficult once the moratorium was over.

One of the worst effects of a moratorium would be the suffering of patients who might be helped by research. As one advocate group advises, "Just ask anybody who suffers

Using Adult DNA: Possible Hope?

Therapeutic cloning using stem cells currently appears to be the approach having the most predictable and positive results. Embryonic stem cells, by their nature, are capable of developing to serve many particular functions. However, some researchers are also looking at adult, or somatic, cells. Remember, all cells in an organism contain the full genome—a copy of the entire DNA "recipe book" for making all of the organism's proteins, not just the ones usually produced by a given cell. That means, theoretically, that genes transferred from any cell should work. This technique, known as somatic cell nuclear transfer (SCNT), represents a highly useful line of research. The good news is that embryonic stem cells are not required. The bad news is that the results are less certain. But, SCNT may offer the greatest hope for the nearly 100 million Americans who suffer from cancer, Alzheimer's disease, diabetes, Parkinson's disease, spinal cord injuries, heart disease, ALS (amyotrophic lateral sclerosis or Lou Gehrig's disease), and other serious, chronic conditions for which treatments have not yet been found.

Human Therapeutic Cloning

Person

Somatic cell biopsy

Enucleated donor oocyte

Nuclear transfer

Embryonic stem cells

Pancreatic islet cells

Hematopoietic cells

Cardiomyocytes

Neurons

Hepatocytes

Immunologically Compatible Transplant

from Parkinson's or anyone who cares for someone with Alzheimer's whether they are willing to wait."

Dr. Leon Kass, the University of Chicago professor who is chairman of the Bioethics Council established by President George W. Bush, disagrees. He said as he submitted the Council's July 2002 report, "The Senate will do what it will, but I hope this report rekindles an interest in finding a way around the impasse," referring to the deadlock in Congress that summer. "A moratorium on all human cloning so that the debate can continue—I think that would be a wonderful conclusion."

Reagan and Reeve: Close to the Issue

Among the many advocates who speak out on the question of therapeutic cloning, two are especially poignant for their closeness to the issue: Nancy Reagan and Christopher Reeve.

For some time, and especially since 1994, Nancy Reagan has watched her husband's memory deteriorate through the ravages of Alzheimer's disease. In happier years, Ronald Reagan had served two terms, from 1981 to 1988, as the fortieth president of the United States, becoming the first and only actor to be elected to that office. Today, Ronald Reagan no longer recognizes members of his family. Nancy Reagan, always a strong advocate for what she thinks is right, has taken a position in opposition to George W. Bush, even though she helped campaign for his father (who was vice president under Reagan and later president). Now she campaigns for stem cell research because she firmly believes that it might find an effective treatment for Alzheimer's. She disagrees with President Bush, but she complains quietly because she does not want

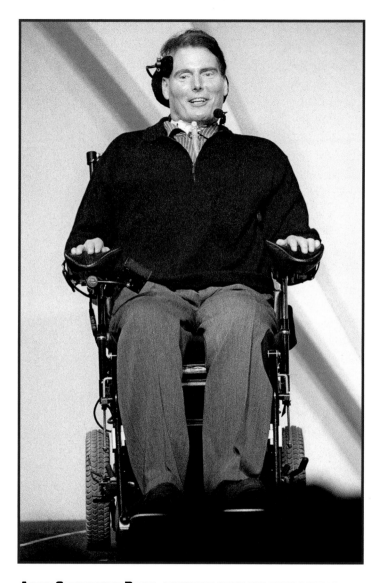

ACTOR CHRISTOPHER REEVE, PARALYZED FROM THE NECK DOWN BY
A FALL FROM A HORSE, DELIVERS SPEECHES IN FAVOR OF STEM CELL
RESEARCH, WHICH MAY EVENTUALLY HELP OTHERS LIKE HIM RECOVER
SOME LOST ABILITIES. HERE, HE IS SPEAKING TO A BIOTECHNOLOGY
CONFERENCE HELD IN BOSTON IN 2000.

to seem un-Republican in her opposition to the president's stand. She was quoted in *The New York Times* as saying to a friend, "A lot of time is being wasted. A lot of people who could be helped are not being helped." News reports say Reagan has contacted twenty members of Congress and talked to members of the administration. She has discussed the matter with several leading scientists, including former director of the National Cancer Institute, Dr. Richard D. Klausner. She also wrote to Bush in 2001, telling him that she hoped her husband's legacy might include sparing other families what hers has suffered. She has continued to make her feelings known through friends.

Another strong critic of Bush and advocate of stem cell research is former actor Christopher Reeve, who is paralyzed from the neck down resulting from a fall he took while horseback riding in 1995. As an actor, Reeve is best known for his role as Superman. Reeve has said that if stem cell research had been encouraged sooner, a treatment for his spinal cord injury might have already been found and might now be nearing the stage of trials on human patients.

In Reeve's case, he says that he suffers from "something called demyelination. And that means that, in one very small segment of my spinal cord, about the width of your pinky, the coating, myelin, which is like the rubber coating around a wire, has come off. And that keeps signals from the brain from getting down into the body." He goes on to explain that human embryonic stem cells could be cultured to do a specific job. Then they could be sent directly to the site where the problem exists, "and they would know that their job is to remyelinate." Then, he says, the signals from the brain would get through to the rest of his body the way they are supposed to, and he could recover his ability to move.

What about critics who say that all this is just theory—

that paralysis like Reeve's and the degeneration that takes place in ALS have never been corrected using stem cell therapy? Reeve points out that it has been done by a team of researchers at Johns Hopkins on rats with a simulated ALS-like disease. The rats were injected with human stem cells, and they recovered from the degenerative process that had begun.

"I believe that any reasonable person who is willing to listen to both sides of the argument can be convinced that it is possible to be pro-life and pro-stem cell research at the same time," Christopher Reeve remarked in July 2001. "This issue affects the whole American family, and if we think of ourselves as a family with 250 million members, then I think compassion for our brothers and sisters, parents and children, will lead us to the right conclusion."

Kyla Dunn, a science writer and former biotech researcher says:

To be clear: the embryos scientists intend to use for therapeutic cloning are approximately five days into their development in a lab dish. At this stage, a human embryo is a round, fluid-filled ball of about 150 undifferentiated cells. It is smaller than a grain of sand. It is smaller than the period at the end of this sentence. It would fit effortlessly on the point of a pin. Some people look at that embryo and see a human being. Others look at that same embryo and see just a clump of cells. . . . It all boils down to a pair of maddening insoluble questions: "When does human life begin?" and "At what point does that life deserve society's protection?"

Dunn also points out that embryos like the ones used in therapeutic cloning are commonly created at fertility clinics and used for research or clinical purposes. When a clinic has more than needed, excess embryos may be discarded. In this case, early embryos in a lab dish do not receive the same rights as human beings walking down the street or cuddling in a mother's arms.

Depending on religious and philosophical beliefs, each individual will have different answers to these questions and different reactions to these facts. Dialogue must take place, but one side is not very likely to persuade the other.

However, we as a society need to address these facts soberly in our debates and decisions. Important medical research hangs in the balance. As Reeve and Reagan so poignantly show, almost everyone knows someone who suffers from Alzheimer's, a catastrophic neck injury, Parkinson's, ALS, or another disease or condition that might be cured by this research. Should all these people suffer for the heightened sensibilities of some? Dunn concludes, "Those who are ethically opposed to human-embryo research may choose, for themselves and for their families, not to make use of any cures that arise. But to deny those cures to the rest of us, in my opinion, is simply unconscionable." Dunn is admittedly biased, and this issue runs deep. Other conflicts between differing ethics exist in our culture—for example, the conflict over abortion between those who take a pro-life position and those who are pro-choice. The same question lies at the crux of the conflict: When does an embryo become a human life?

Stem Cell Research: For and Against

Research using human stem cells presents one of the two most controversial aspects of all genetic engineering. Both sides, pro and con, present some strong arguments.

Pluses:

• **Eliminating genetic diseases.** Carefully performed screening programs might eliminate genetic diseases such as Huntington's disease and hemophilia. Ultimately, gene therapy could also help remove genetic diseases from the gene pool.

• **Screening parents or unborn babies for genetic disorders.** Either before pregnancy begins, or during the early months, genetic information could help prospective parents know the risks and make choices about treatment or even birth.

• **Treatments for genetically caused diseases have already been found**—such as prostate cancer, genetically caused infertility, types of leukemia, "bubble boy" syndrome, Parkinson's, **ALS**, and others.

• **Addressing the ethical issues surrounding stem cell research, the Coalition for the Advancement of Medical Research (CAMR), a scientific advocate group,** sees the question of whether or not a child is created the watershed between ethical and unethical cloning. In therapeutic cloning there is no fertilization of the egg by sperm, no implantation in a uterus, no pregnancy, and no child. That would be reproductive cloning, which, according to this group, would be wrong. These scientists and advocates believe that "implantation into a womb is the clear, bright line that divides reproductive and non-reproductive technologies. Without implantation, no new human life is possible." For them, therefore, no ethical dilemma exists.

Minuses:

- Concern remains that gene therapy is risky. In 1999, an eighteen-year-old boy named Jesse Gelsinger died while taking part in a study at the University of Pennsylvania. His death occurred four days after researchers injected him with a genetic drug designed to repair a problem with his liver. Since then, researchers have been more cautious than ever with trials, and that's why they ended the "bubble boy" trials so abruptly.

- For many people, the even greater concern is that cells in their original form are destroyed in the process of therapeutic cloning. Many people see these cells as human lives. From that point of view, destroying one human life to save another is unethical. One ethicist maintains that if DNA is present then you have a cell, and that is a form of human life.

- Others contend that the embryo is never allowed to develop beyond five or six days. Consisting of only about 150 cells and as tiny as a period, this embryo has not yet become human, they argue, so no ethical problem exists. Opponents of this line of reasoning fear that it embarks on a slippery slope that would translate easily into condoning reproductive cloning or destruction of older, more developed embryos.

8

Human Cloning

DOLLY WAS LUCKY

Scientists warn that cloning is too dangerous for people

Science News, October 20, 2001

Most of the public, researchers, and government officials agree that human reproductive cloning might easily spiral out of control. Consider the possibility of "designer babies." What happens if an individual with money decides to buy a copy of himself or herself? The American Association for the Advancement of Science (AAAS), one of the most powerful scientific groups in the United States, consistently supports the advancement of scientific knowledge. However, they think cloning humans is a different matter.

Even those researchers who are most eager to pursue the possible benefits of cloning animals and of therapeutic cloning for humans do not recommend reproductive cloning of humans. The second cloned ewe, born after Dolly at

Roslin Institute, should stand as a warning. Researcher Ian Wilmut echoed the feelings of most of his colleagues when he asked, "Who would [want to] be responsible for a child born with an abnormality like that?" Cloned animals frequently have severe, even fatal, physical problems. In November 2001, Wilmut pointed out that 73 percent of clone pregnancies in a study of calf cloning ended in abortion and 20 percent of those that were born died shortly after birth.

Don Wolf, who works at the Oregon Regional Primate Research Center in Beaverton, agrees. "Based on the plausible outcomes, it's ridiculous to move forward with human cloning." Wolf is working on cloning monkeys, but he says of cloning humans, "It's totally irresponsible."

In August 2001, a meeting of the National Academy of Sciences (NAS), a select body of distinguished and respected scientists and engineers, focused on whether human cloning was possible. The meeting was often emotional. Scientists described both their successes and failures with cloning humans. Most of them concluded that cloning humans was unsafe.

Other scientists think that the emphasis on failed clones is misplaced. In vitro fertilizations (IVF or "test tube babies") also have often failed early in development. Also, fewer IVF human babies than IVF animals have problems once they are born. So, these scientists reason, perhaps some of the research already done on cloning animals is irrelevant to humans.

At the NAS meeting, in fact, three scientists said they intended to go ahead with plans to attempt human cloning. One of those scientists, Brigitte Boisselier, chemist and director of the biotechnology firm Clonaid, asserted, "I believe it's a fundamental right to reproduce the way

White House Directive

Immediately after the announcement of Dolly's birth in February 1997, U.S. President Bill Clinton sent the following letter to the Chair of the National Bioethics Advisory Commission. Clinton's quick action and the tone of his letter reflect the seriousness with which the issues were viewed at the time, as they are still today.

THE WHITE HOUSE
WASHINGTON
February 24, 1997
Dr. Harold Shapiro
Chair
National Bioethics Advisory Commission
Suite 3C01
6100 Executive Boulevard
Bethesda, Maryland 20892-7508

Dear Dr. Shapiro:

As you know, it was reported today that researchers have developed techniques to clone sheep. This represents a remarkable scientific discovery, but one that raises important questions. While this technological advance could offer potential benefits in such areas as medical research and agriculture, it also raises serious ethical questions, particularly with respect to the possible use of this technology to clone human embryos.

Therefore, I request that the National Bioethics Advisory Commission undertake a thorough review of the legal and ethical issues associated with the use of this technology, and report back to me within ninety days with recommendations on possible federal actions to prevent its abuse.

Sincerely,

Bill Clinton

BRIGITTE BOISSELIER, WHO HOLDS TWO DOCTORATES IN CHEMISTRY, IS MANAGING DIRECTOR OF CLONAID, THE FIRST FIRM IN THE WORLD TO CLAIM THE BIRTH OF A HUMAN CLONE. THE CLONING, HOWEVER, WAS NOT CONFIRMED, AND MOST SERIOUS SCIENTISTS DOUBT IT WAS SUCCESSFUL. BOISSELIER IS ALSO A BISHOP IN THE RAELIAN RELIGIOUS SECT, WHOSE FOUNDER ASSERTS HE HAS BEEN IN CONTACT WITH AN EXTRATERRESTRIAL BEING WHO CLAIMS THAT HUMANS WERE CLONED FROM BEINGS FROM ANOTHER PLANET 25,000 YEARS AGO.

you want." Her organization's expertise, however, has since come under question.

The other two scientists, Italian reproductive researcher Severino Antinori, who directs a fertility clinic in Rome and Panos Zavos of the Andrology Institute of America (which studies male sexual and reproductive disorders) in Lexington, Kentucky, think they will have better luck with humans than animal researchers have had with cloning animals. With multiple safeguards in place, they think human cloning could be safe and successful.

However, researchers involved in therapeutic uses of cloning fear a backlash against their work because of the public reaction to plans made by Antinori and Zavos. The Biotechnology Industry Organization, which represents biotech industry interests, wrote a letter to President Bush immediately after the announcement. The organization's bioethics counsel, Michael Warner, explained the group's position, "We think it's unethical and inappropriate and dangerous to clone human beings at this point. . . . But the use of cloning technology has the potential to be enormously beneficial and should not be lost."

An even greater brouhaha played out in the newspapers in December 2002 when news media around the world reported that Clonaid, the company founded by the Raelian sect, claimed to have produced the first human clone. Brigitte Boisselier, the chemist who had earlier announced the Raelians' intentions to proceed with their experiments in human cloning, told the press that the seven-pound baby girl named Eve, produced from skin cells taken from her thirty-one-year-old American mother, was healthy and doing well. The birth was said to have taken place in an undisclosed location outside the United States.

Needless to say the announcement sent shockwaves across the media. Television, radio, and newspapers carried the story, often in sensational terms. But scientists were deeply skeptical of the Raelian claims.

Many scientists expressed doubts that the Raelian sect, a strange group that believes that all life on Earth was a product of genetic engineering by the hands of extraterrestrials and that Jesus Christ was resurrected by advanced cloning procedures, had the technical knowledge or capabilities to have performed such a feat. Scientists around the world waited for the proof that the Raelians promised would come in a few days after the announcement.

The Raeliens claimed that the proof would come in the form of DNA tests to be performed by neutral parties. These tests would establish that the baby was indeed a clone of its mother. While the world waited for the arrangements to be made for the testing, anti-cloning activists jumped on the story that, if confirmed, would exceed their worst fears. Even the "kooks," it seemed, could get into the cloning business and produce human clones!

Equally troubled were the scientists, ethicists, and politicians engaged in serious debate over the merits and demerits of stem cell research and human cloning. While most doubted the truth of the announcement, its sheer sensationalism raised the passions of much of the public, which made reasonable debate of the difficult subject even more difficult.

Then, almost as quickly as the story burst across the media, it began to fizzle. The announced trip to America by "baby Eve" and her mother to allow DNA samples to be taken was suddenly canceled. Official announcements from Clonaid and the Raelians claimed that the child's family, disturbed by the publicity and increasing invasions of their privacy, had decided against performing the DNA tests. According to later reports from the Raelians, the baby and her family had gone to an undisclosed place in

Israel to escape from the intrusions into their privacy. Both mother and baby, said the Raelians, were doing well. And there was still hope, Clonaid spokespeople said, that the family would eventually permit the necessary testing to establish the proof that "baby Eve" was indeed the world's first human clone.

As of early 2003, no such tests had been performed. Although Clonaid and the Raelians have announced the birth of yet another human clone, the child of a Dutch lesbian couple, no scientific proof has been offered that either child was cloned or, in fact, even existed.

In the United States, religious, moral, and ethical considerations have taken precedence over most of the discussion of safety in human cloning, and a moratorium or outright ban on the practice is currently under consideration by the United Nations. However, Panos Zavos told ABC News, "If we don't do it, somebody else will do it, and they'll do it soon and probably in a very irresponsible way."

Human Reproductive Cloning: Positive or Negative?

Pluses

- **Proponents point out that many improvements in human life can result from cloning, including more intelligent babies, longer and healthier lives, and new freedoms for parents such as the right to choose their child's gender.**

- **Development of this technology is potentially beneficial. By outlawing human cloning, the United States** may effectively drive the technology out of the country, possibly encouraging more unethical uses elsewhere in the world.

• **Driving human cloning out of the United States will not make it unavailable, but in effect will probably end up reserving the technology for those wealthy enough to buy it.**

• **Reproduction would no longer require sexual intercourse, overcoming many barriers faced by couples having reproductive or sexual inabilities.**

• **We cannot answer in advance all the questions about what will happen but proponents point out that the existence of potential problems should not be allowed to block development. Instead, they suggest, the technology should be allowed to develop with caution. Then concerned bioethicists can address problems about how it will be used as they come up. Couples may try to control other traits besides those that are clearly harmful. What if they want to select the sex of their baby? That seems reasonable, but then will there be too many boys? Or too many girls? Biomedical reproductive clinics could be required to keep an overall balance as a condition of their licensing. But what if couples make irresponsible, trendy choices that are not in the best interest of their children? Girls with green hair, for example?**

• Biomedical research will lead to cures for many genetic defects, such as an inherited chemical imbalance that leads to mental retardation. Solutions may be found for curing or preventing Alzheimer's, heart disease, and cancer, but to find these solutions one must unravel biology and encourage the development of the technologies required. By eliminating such disorders, inequities may be reduced between the haves and have-nots.

• This is the next natural step in human evolution. Gregory Stock, director of the UCLA Program on Medicine, Science, and Technology and author of *Redesigning Humans: Our Inevitable Genetic Future,* says that only the most extreme totalitarian government could dissuade people from pursuing these technologies, so great would be the benefits gained from human reproductive cloning—and so enormous the losses from not pursuing its development.

• Reproductive cloning may provide a safer mode of reproduction than sexual reproduction—putting children less at risk for genetic disorders. Things are more likely to go wrong in natural sexual reproduction, which sometimes results in children who are born malformed, mentally or emotionally.

Minuses

• Many people worry that we do not know enough about this new technology and what may happen—either from a scientific or a sociological point of view.

• We may be trying to play too big a role (God's role, from a religious viewpoint) in the universe and in human lives. We may not be wise enough or smart enough to avoid negative outcomes.

• Human reproductive cloning may always be available only to the rich. But if market forces are allowed to

Points of View

Arguments about genetic engineering are as diverse as the people who uphold them, and much of what someone believes is based on that person's world view. Recognizing the influence of an individual's grounding or beliefs can be key to understanding a person's arguments. For example:

- **An environmentalist will probably be concerned about issues such as species diversity and preservation of naturally evolved genetics. Some environmentalists call for extreme tactics against planting genetically modified (GM) crops, for example. Other environmentalists disagree with this approach, even though they may otherwise agree with the general world view.**

- **Many people with strong religious beliefs object to genetic engineering as an interference with God's creation. Even those who are comfortable with other forms of engineering, medicine, food preservatives, and so on, may not be comfortable with manipulating genes—or they may object to some forms of genetic modification and not others.**

• Those concerned with world hunger and conditions in underdeveloped countries may campaign for making inexpensive, nutritious food as widely available as possible.

• Farmers and agricultural scientists may support the development of GM crops that are easier and more economical to grow.

• Physicians and health specialists may be eager to make available the many therapeutic advantages that genetic engineering can provide—in dozens of ways.

• Politicians tend to respond to the opinions of those who vote for them, as well as acting from their own convictions.

• Scientists engaged in genetic engineering usually believe that their work will benefit people and add to the general well-being of the world. Of course, they also may have strong personal reasons for promoting genetic engineering—since their ability to continue their research depends on its acceptance.

drive biomedical research, the rich will perpetuate their social advantages by controlling the genetics of their children.

• In the opinion of many bioethicists, even within the biotechnology industry, cloning a human being at this stage of research in particular is irresponsible.

• In a report entitled "Cloning Human Beings" submitted to President Clinton in June 1997, the National Bioethics Advisory Commission stated that the prospect of creating children from a single cell prompted "serious safety concerns," as well as issues regarding "individuality, family integrity, and treating children as objects."

• No existing social structure is currently prepared to handle the broad and complex sociological and ethical challenge presented by human cloning. In a comment for a *Religion and Ethics Newsweekly* article on the Council on Bioethics on January 18, 2002, political scientist Francis Fukuyama of Johns Hopkins remarked, "You're going to have all sorts of issues coming up in the future: Should we allow parents to select enhancement characteristics in their children? Right now there's no regulatory structure that will allow you to make that kind of a decision. The more important issues go beyond the immediate cloning thing."

Conclusion

Peter Medawar was right when he said that the development of genetic engineering has rivaled the advent of nuclear warheads for its ability to rouse dismay and fear of threats both imagined and real. Yet this infant field of research holds great promise for advances in health and medicine. It holds out hope for advancements in agriculture, manufacturing, and invention. It offers food for starving millions. At the same time, it justifies many of our fears and severely tests human wisdom and understanding. It challenges human governments and individuals with the need to move forward with caution, recognizing the very real and complex ethical and social issues that this technology brings to the years ahead.

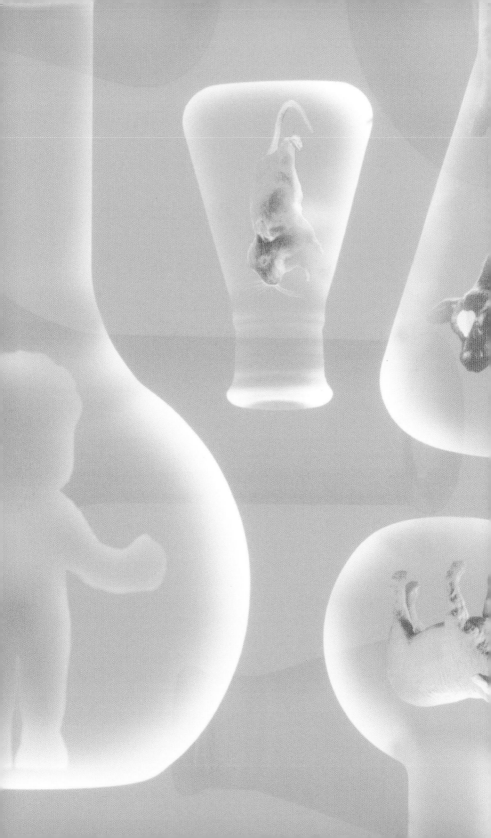

Notes

Chapter 1

p. 10, As the noted British biologist Peter Brian Medawar remarked . . . : Peter Brian Medawar, quoted by *The New York Review of Books*, October 27, 1977, cited by James D. Watson and John Tooze in *The DNA Story: A Documentary History of Gene Cloning*. New York: W. H. Freeman Co., 1983, p. 243.

pp. 18–19, "The Four Fundamental Pillars of Genetics.": Alan McHughen. *Pandora's Picnic Basket: The Potential and Hazards of Genetically Modified Foods*. New York: Oxford University Press, 2000, p. 27.

Chapter 2

pp. 24–25, "We have approached our review . . .": Brad Stone. Food and Drug Administration Press Release. http://www.fda.gov/bbs/topics/NEWS/NEW00482.html (Accessed March 3, 2003.) Also: Access Excellence, The National Health Museum: About Biotech. "The Flavr Savr Arrives." May 18, 1994.

www.accessexcellence.org/AB/BA/Flavr_Savr_Arrives.
html (Accessed March 3, 2003.)

p. 25, 27–28, In September 2000, GM crops hit the news
headlines . . .: FDA/Office of Public Affairs. "StarLink
Corn Investigation and Recall." Updated on March 1, 2001.
http://www.fda.gov/fdac/features/2001/201_food.html
(Accessed June 26, 2002.)

Chapter 3

p. 38, He wonders how "Mr. Happy's Hot Dog Stand" . . . :
Alan McHughen. *Pandora's Picnic Basket: The Potential
and Hazards of Genetically Modified Foods.* New York:
Oxford University Press, 2000, p. 217.

p. 38, In early October 2002, . . . : Paul Elias. "Labeling
Sets Off a Food Fight." *Sacramento Bee.* October 5, 2002, p. D1.

p. 40, "Constant media coverage . . .": McHughen, p. 263.

Chapter 4

p. 45, What is the connection between trees . . .: Quebec
Forest Industries Association. "The Paper: To Learn
Even More." http://www.aifq.qc.ca/english/machine/
machine.html (Accessed March 1, 2003.)

Chapter 5

p. 52, On May 2, 2002, Cynthia Batchelder . . .: Edie Lau.
"Cloned Calf 'healthy and aggressive' at UC Davis."
Sacramento Bee. May 9, 2002, p. B5.

p. 57, If a species is dying out . . . : Bijal P. Trivedi.
"Scientists Clone First Endangered Species: a Wild
Sheep." *National Geographic Today.* http://news.
nationalgeographic.com/news/2001/10/1025_TV
sheepclone.html (Accessed November 7, 2002.)

p. 59, Ecosystem processes . . . : Adapted from
Environment Australia: Biodiversity Home Page.
http://www.ea.gov.au/biodiversity/index.html (Accessed
November 9, 2002.)

p. 61, Animal science professor Joy Mench . . . :
Leavenworth, Stuart. "New Cloning Fears Raised; Food
from Engineered Animals around Since '80s." *Sacramento
Bee*, August 21, 2002, p. A1.

p. 63, "We humans care more about animals . . .":
Charles, Dan, in "Profile: FDA Turns to the National
Academy of Sciences about Concerns Surrounding
Genetically Engineered Animals." Transcript: *Morning
Edition*, NPR, August 21, 2002.

Chapter 6

p. 70, In 1990, teams of scientists . . . : Human Genome
Project Information. http://www.ornl.gov/hgmis
(Accessed November 10, 2002.)

p. 72, Let patients know . . . :   Human Genome
Project Information. "June 25, 2000: President Clinton
Announces the Completion of the First Survey of the
Entire Human Genome . . . "The White House, Office
of the Press Secretary." http://www.ornl.gov/
TechResources/Human_Genome/project/clinton1.html
(Accessed April 1, 2003.)

p. 73, Researchers have had good success . . . : Memorial
Sloan-Kettering Cancer Center. "Chronic Myelogenous
Leukemia:Treatment." http://www.mskcc.org/mskcc/
html/5467.cfm (Accessed November 10, 2002.)

p. 73, "For the first time . . .": American Cancer Society.
"Major Developments in Cancer Research 2001."
http://www.cancer.org/docroot/RES/content/
RES_7_4_Major_Developments_in_Cancer_Research.
asp?sitearea=RES (Accessed November 10, 2002.)

Chapter 7

p. 82, "The Senate will do what it will . . .": Aaron Zeitner, "THE NATION: Panel Favors Cloning Moratorium but Not Ban." *Los Angeles Times*, July 12, 2002, p. A11.

pp. 82, 84–85, For some time, and especially since 1994 . . . : Alessandra Stanley. "Nancy Reagan, Bush Divided by Stem Cell Issue." *Sacramento Bee*, September 29, 2002, p. A21.

p. 84–85, Another strong critic . . . : CNN.com. "Christopher Reeve on Politics and Stem Cell Research." http://www.cnn.com/2001/ALLPOLITICS/07/29/ reeve.cnna (Accessed January 21, 2002.)

p. 85, "I believe that any reasonable . . .": About.com. "Chris Reeve, President Bush, and Stem Cell Research." http://backandneck.about.com/library/weekly/ aa071701a.htm (Accessed October 2, 2002.)

pp. 85–86, "To be clear: the embryos . . ." Kyla Dunn. "The Life (and Death?) of Cloning." *The Atlantic* online: Atlantic Unbound. May 22, 2002. http://www. theatlantic.com/unbound/interviews/int2002-05-22. htm (Accessed June 2, 2002.)

Chapter 8

p. 90, "Who would [want to] be responsible . . .": John Travis. "Dolly Was Lucky." *Science News*. vol. 160, no. 16, October 20, 2001, p. 250. http://www.sciencenews.org/ 20011020/bob15.asp (Accessed April 1, 2003.)

p. 90, In November 2001 . . . : Emma Young. "Dolly the Sheep Has Arthritis." NewScientist.com. January 4, 2002. http://www.newscientist.com (Accessed January 5, 2002.)

p. 90, "Based on the plausible outcomes . . .": John Travis. Ibid.

p. 93, "We think it's unethical . . .": Onion, Amanda. "Cloning's Two Sides." ABCNEWS.com. February 15, 2001. http://abcnews.go.com/sections/scitech/ DailyNews/cloning010216.html (Accessed January 14, 2002.)

p. 95, "If we don't do it . . .": Ibid.

p. 97, This is the next natural . . . : Katharine Mieszkowski. "Our Shiny Happy Clone Future." Interview with Gregory Stock, director of the UCLA Program on Medicine, Science and Technology, and author of *Redesigning Humans: Our Inevitable Genetic Future*. http://archive.salon.com/tech/ feature/2002/05/28/goodclones/index1.html (Accessed April 29, 2003.)

p. 100, No existing social structure . . . : Kass, Leon. "Leon Kass, chairman, President's Council on Bioethics: On Human Cloning." News, Council on Bioethics. http://www.pbs.org/wnet/religionandethics/ week520/kass.html (Accessed March 2, 2003.)

Further Information

Further Reading

Boon, Kevin Alexander. *The Human Genome Project: What Does Decoding DNA Mean for Us?* Berkeley Heights, NJ: Enslow Publishers, 2002.

Cohen, Daniel. *Cloning.* rev. ed. Brookfield, CT: Twenty-First Century Books, 2002.

Duprau, Jeanne. *Cloning.* Lucent Overview Series. San Diego, CA: Lucent Books, 2000.

Freedman, Jeri. *Everything You Need to Know about Genetically Modified Foods*. Need to Know Library. New York: Rosen Publishing Group, 2003.

Gonick, Larry, and Mark Wheelis. *Cartoon Guide to Genetics*. rev. ed. New York: HarperCollins Publishers, 1991.

Goodnough, David. *The Debate over Human Cloning: A Pro/Con Issue*. Berkeley Heights, NJ: Enslow Publishers, Inc., 2003.

Judson, Karen. *Genetic Engineering*. Issues in Focus Series. Berkeley Heights, NJ: Enslow Publishers, Inc., 2001.

Kowalski, Kathiann M. *The Debate over Genetically Engineered Foods: Healthy or Harmful?* Issues in Focus. Berkeley Heights, NJ: Enslow Publishers, Inc., 2002.

Web Sites

National Center for Biotechnology Information
http://www.ncbi.nlm.nih.gov

This site is maintained by the U.S. National Library of Medicine and the National Institutes of Health. It promotes better understanding of molecular processes that affect human health and disease.

Access Excellence
http://www.accessexcellence.org

This National Health Museum site for health and bioscience teachers and learners includes a section called "About Biotech" that explores issues and ethics, uses of biotechnology, biotech careers, and a graphics gallery.

Bioethics for Beginners
http://bioethics.net/beginners.php

An extensive site by the *American Journal of Bioethics*, including "An Introduction to Bioethics," an overview of the history and impact of bioethics on today's society, and "Help with Your Homework," for students working on a bioethics project.

Biotechnology Online Secondary School Resource
http://www.biotechnology.gov.au/biotechnologyOnline/

A service of the Australian government, this Web site objectively discusses biotechnology and the associated issues.

The Center for Bioethics: Who Owns Life?
http://www.med.upenn.edu/bioethic/wol

The University of Pennsylvania School of Medicine explores the question "Who owns life?" regarding patented plants (such as Bt corn) and animals.

Genetic Engineering
http://www.sierraclub.org/biotech

The Sierra Club discusses its position against the use of genetic engineering, including articles on genetically engineered trees, genetic contamination, protests against GE crops and food, and agricultural biotechnology in a hungry world.

Bibliography

About.com. "Chris Reeve, President Bush, and Stem Cell Research." http://backandneck.about.com/library/weekly/aa071701a.htm (Accessed October 2, 2002.)

Alliance for Better Foods, The. "Food for Thought, November 2002." http://www.betterfoods.org/News/fftnov08.htm (Accessed November 11, 2002.)

American Cancer Society. "Major Developments in Cancer Research 2001." http://www.cancer.org/docroot/RES/content/RES_7_4_Major_Developments_in_Cancer_Research.asp?sitearea=RES (Accessed November 10, 2002.)

BBC News. "Prince Charles speaks out against GM food." http://news.bbc.co.uk/2/hi/special_report/1999/02/99/food_ under_the_microscope/285408.stm (Accessed April 29, 2003.)

CNN.com. "Christopher Reeve on Politics and Stem Cell Research." http://www.cnn.com/2001/ALLPOLITICS/ 07/29/reeve.cnna (Accessed January 21, 2002.)

Dunn, Kyla. "The Life (and Death?) of Cloning." *The Atlantic* Online: Atlantic Unbound. May 22, 2002. http://www.theatlantic.com/unbound/interviews/int2002-05-22.htm. (Accessed June 2, 2002.)

Environment Australia: Biodiversity Home Page. http://www.ea.gov.au/biodiversity/index.html. (Accessed November 9, 2002.)

FDA/Office of Public Affairs. "StarLink Corn Investigation and Recall." Updated on March 1, 2001. http://www.fda.gov/fdac/features/2001/201_food.html (Accessed June 26, 2002.)

Human Genome Project Information. http://www.ornl.gov/hgmis (Accessed November 10, 2002.)

Human Genome Project Information. "June 25, 2000: President Clinton Announces the Completion of the First Survey of the Entire Human Genome . . ." The White House, Office of the Press Secretary. http://www.ornl.gov/TechResources/Human_Genome/proj ect/clinton1.html (Accessed November 10, 2002.)

Kass, Leon. "Leon Kass, Chairman, President's Council on Bioethics: On Human Cloning." Council on Bioethics Web site. http://www.pbs.org/wnet/religionandethics/week520/kass.html (Accessed March 2, 2003.)

Kolata, Gina B. *Clone: The Road to Dolly, and the Path Ahead*. New York: Morrow, 1998.

Lau, Edie. "Cloned calf 'healthy and aggressive' at UC Davis." *Sacramento Bee*, May 9, 2002, p. B5.

Lewis, Ricki A. *Discovery: Windows on the Life Sciences*. Malden, MA: Blackwell Science, 2001.

McGhee, Glenn, ed. *The Human Cloning Debate*, 2nd edition. Berkeley, CA: Berkeley Hills Books, 2000.

McHughen, Alan. *Pandora's Picnic Basket: The Potential and Hazards of Genetically Modified Foods*. New York: Oxford University Press, 2000.

Memorial Sloan-Kettering Cancer Center. "Chronic Myelogenous Leukemia: Treatment." http://www.mskcc.org/mskcc/html/5467.cfm (Accessed November 10, 2002.)

Mieszkowski, Katharine. "Our shiny happy clone future." May 25, 2002. http://www.salon.com/tech/feature/2002/05/28/goodclones/index.html (Accessed April 29, 2003.)

Murray, Thomas H., and Maxwell J. Mehlman, eds. *Encyclopedia of Ethical, Legal, and Policy Issues in Biotechnology.* New York: John Wiley and Sons, 2000.

National Research Council; Committee on Defining Science-Based Concerns Associated with Products of Animal Biotechnology; and Committee on Agricultural Biotechnology, Health, and the Environment. *Animal Biotechnology: Science Based Concerns.* Washington, DC: National Academies Press, 2002.

National Research Council; Committee on Environmental Impacts Associated with Commercialization of Transgenic Plants, Board on Agriculture and Natural Resources. *Environmental Effects of Transgenic Plants: The Scope and Adequacy of Regulation.* Washington, DC: National Academies Press, 2002.

Onion, Amanda. "Cloning's Two Sides" ABCNEWS.com, February 15, 2001. http://abcnews.go.com/sections/scitech/DailyNews/cloning010216.html (Accessed January 14, 2002.)

Pence, Gregory E. *Designer Food: Mutant Harvest or Breadbasket of the World?* New York: Rowman and Littlefield, 2002.

President's Council on Bioethics. *Human Cloning and Human Dignity: An Ethical Inquiry.* Washington, D.C.: Public Affairs Reports, 2002. http://bioethicsprint.bioethics.gov/reports/cloningreport/index.html (Accessed March 2, 2003.)

Quebec Forest Industries Association. "The Paper: To Learn Even More." http://www.aifq.qc.ca/english/machine/machine.html (Accessed March 1, 2003.)

Saunders, William L., J.D., "Calculated Deception: Cloning Advocates Aren't Telling the Truth." http://www.cloninginformation.org/commentaries/05062002/html (Accessed May 7, 2002.)

Stanley, Alessandra. "Nancy Reagan, Bush divided by stem cell issue." *Sacramento Bee*, September 29, 2002, p. A21.

Stone, Brad. Food and Drug Administration Press Release. "P94-10, Flavr Savr Tomato." May 18, 1994. http://www.fda.gov/bbs/topics/NEWS/NEW00482.html (Accessed April 29, 2003.)

Travis, John. "Dolly Was Lucky." *Science News*. vol. 160, no. 16, October 20, 2001, p. 250. http://www.science news.org/20011020/fob1.htm (Accessed January 28, 2002.)

Trivedi, Bijal P. "Scientists Clone First Endangered Species: a Wild Sheep." *National Geographic Today*. http://news.na-tionalgeographic.com/news/2001/10/1025_TVsheepclone.html (Accessed November 7, 2002.)

Watson, James D., and John Tooze. *The DNA Story: A Documentary History of Gene Cloning*. New York: W. H. Freeman Co., 1983.

Wilmut, Ian, Keith Campbell, and Colin Tudge. *The Second Creation: Dolly and the Age of Biological Controls.* New York: Farrar, Straus & Giroux, 2000.

Young, Emma. "Dolly the Sheep Has Arthritis." NewScientist.com. January 4, 2002. http://www.newscientist.com (Accessed January 5, 2002.)

Index

Page numbers in **boldface** are illustrations, tables, and charts.

About the Authors

RAY SPANGENBURG and **KIT MOSER** have coauthored more than fifty books and one hundred articles for teenagers and adults on science, technology, critical thinking, and social issues. Their most recent books include *The Crime of Genocide*, *Propaganda*, and *TV News: Can It Be Trusted?* They are also coauthors of a five-volume history of science and the award-winning biography *Niels Bohr: Gentle Genius of Denmark*.